HOW TO DRAW UNICORNS DOT TO DOT

A STEP-BY-STEP DRAWING AND ACTIVITY BOOK FOR KIDS TO LEARN TO DRAW CUTE STUFF

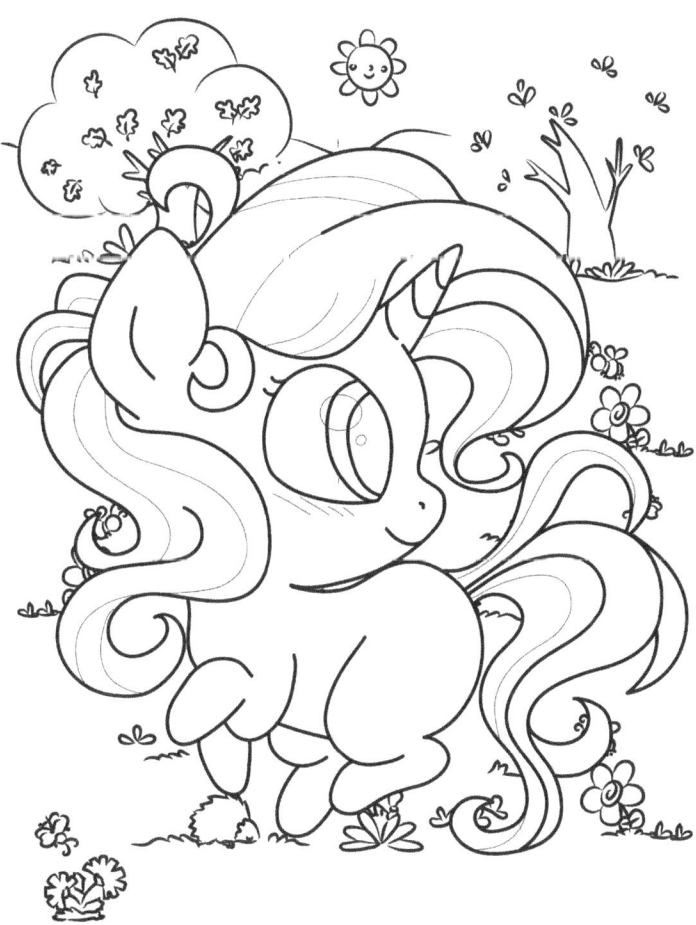

BOOK AND COVER DESIGN BY PHOO PUNYA

ISBN: 9781074877712

FIRST EDITION: JUNE 2019

How To Draw

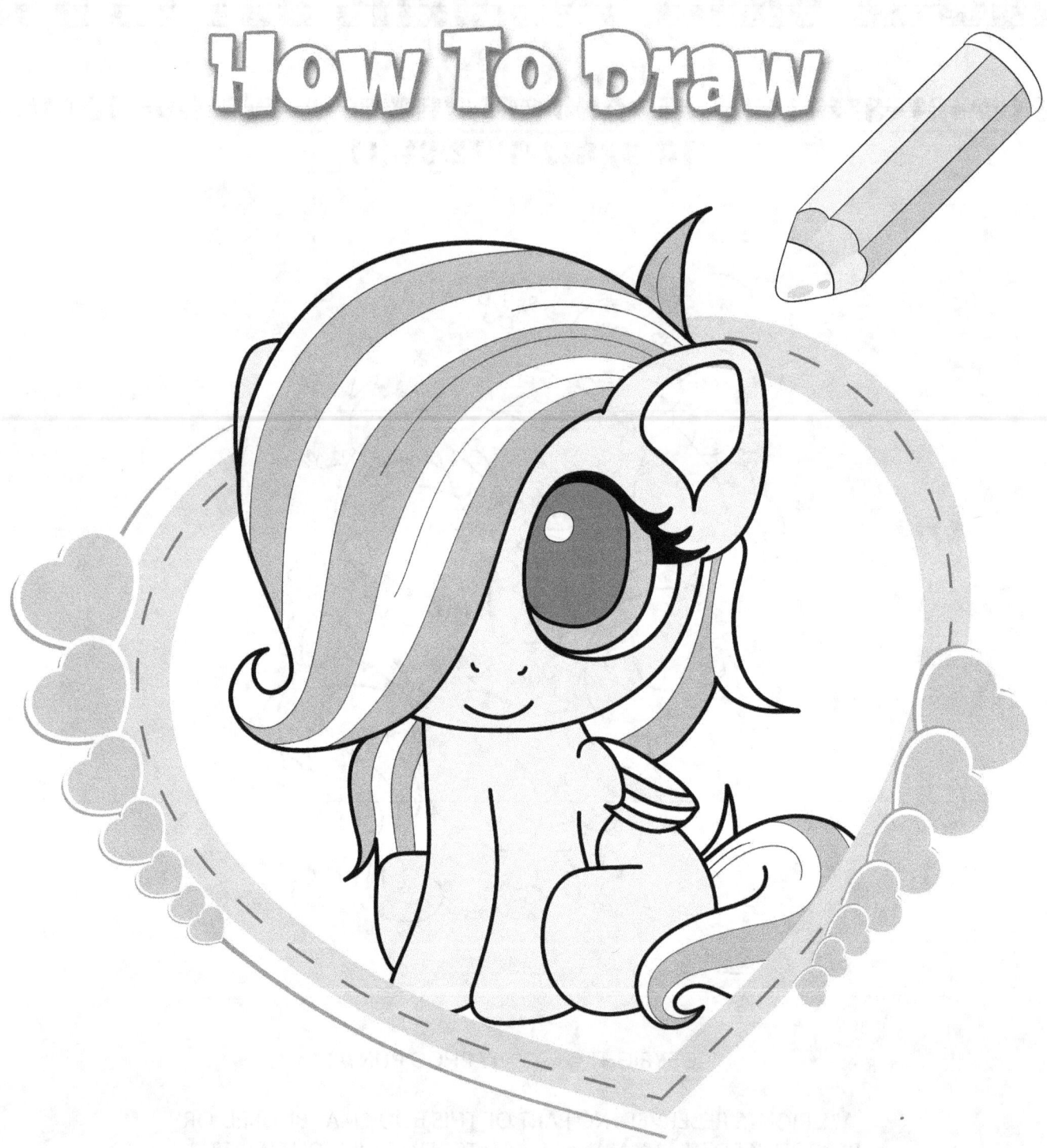

Cute Unicorns

This Book Belongs to :

....

....

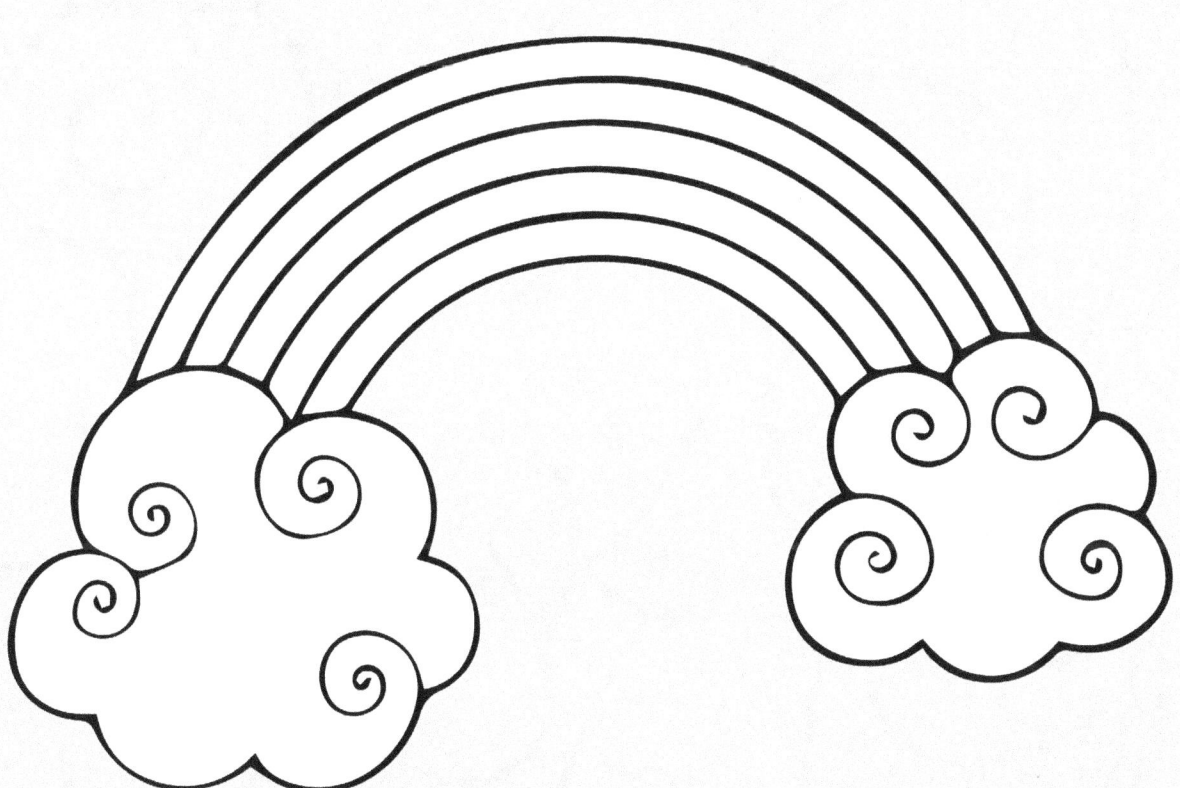

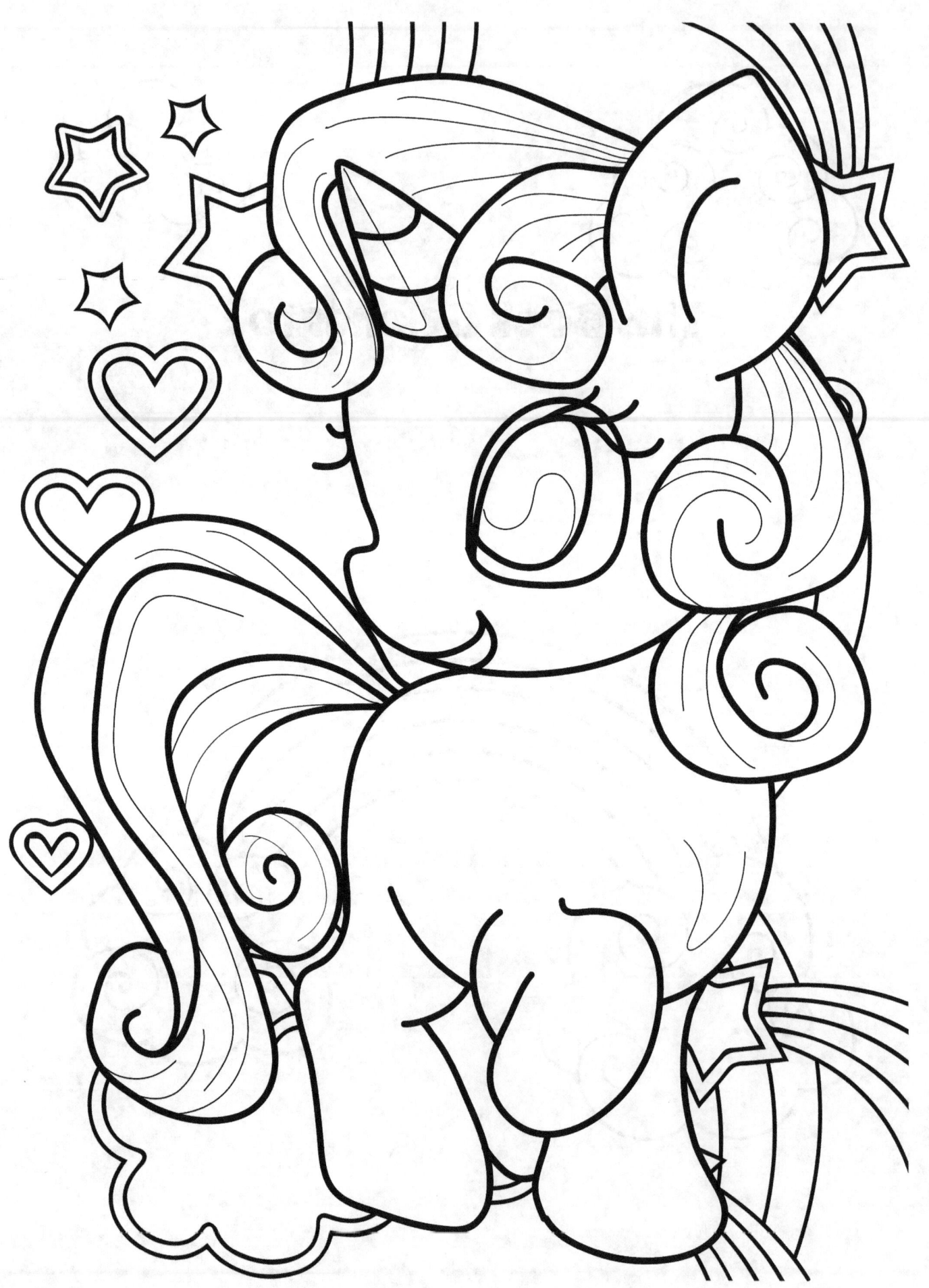

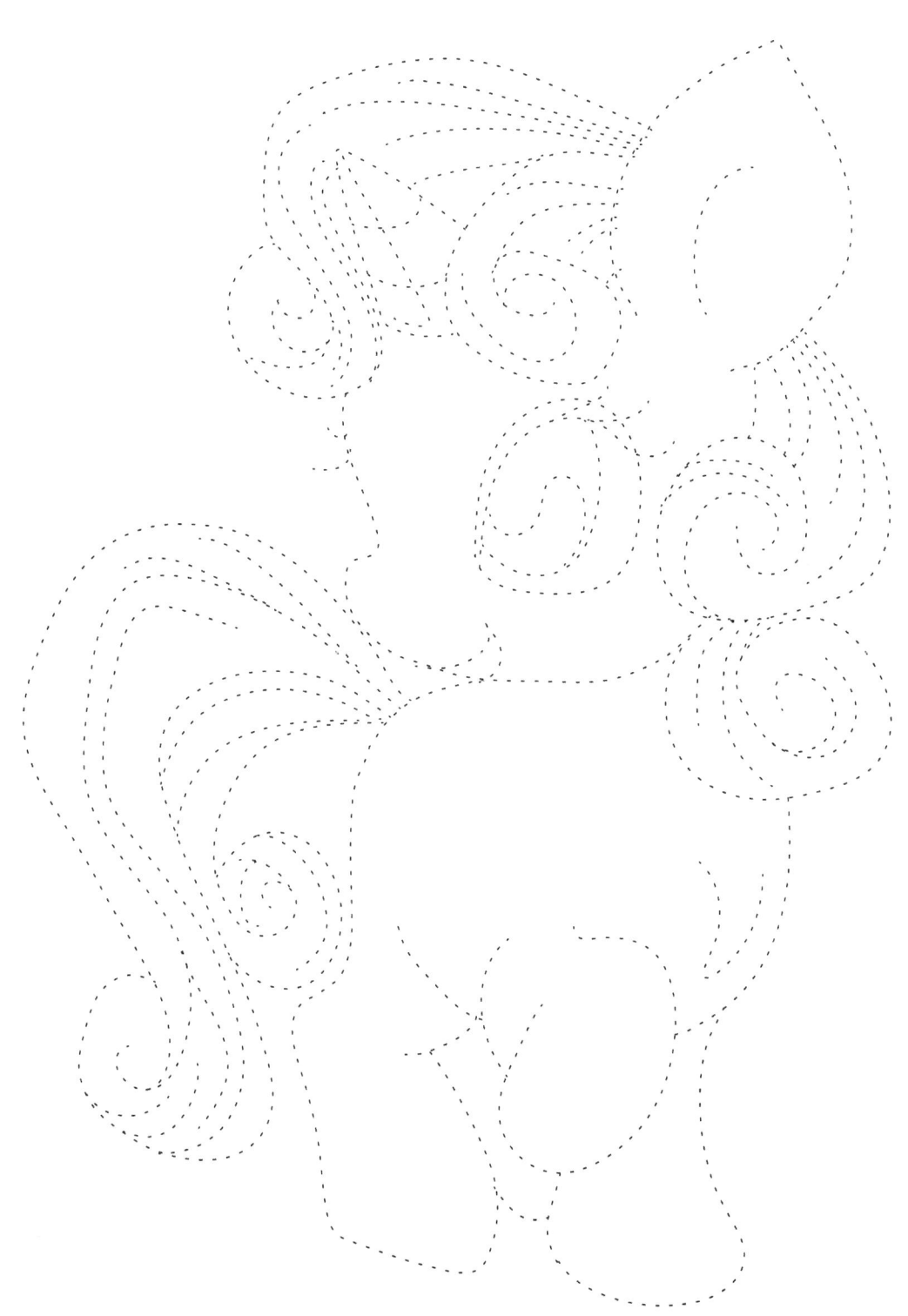

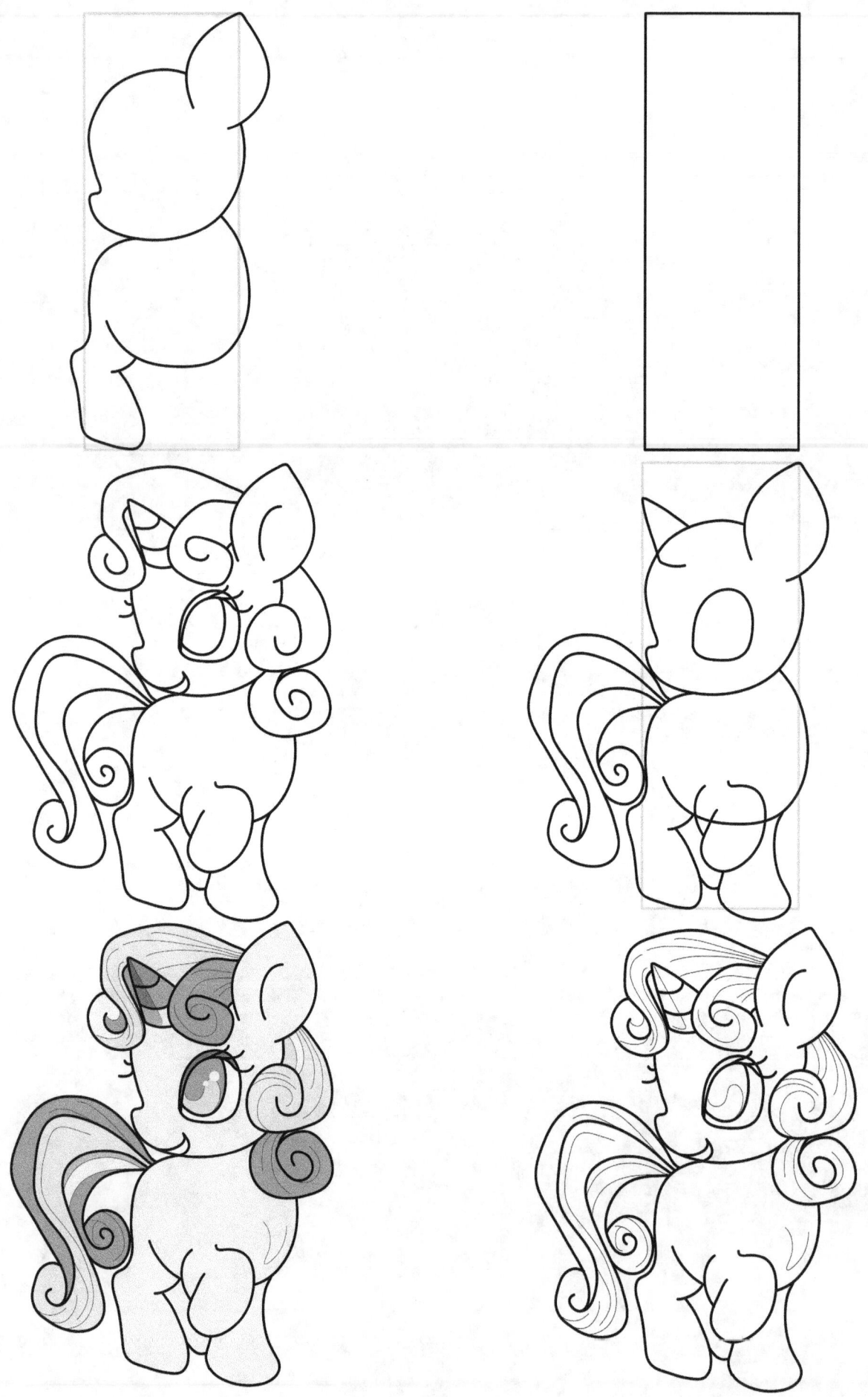

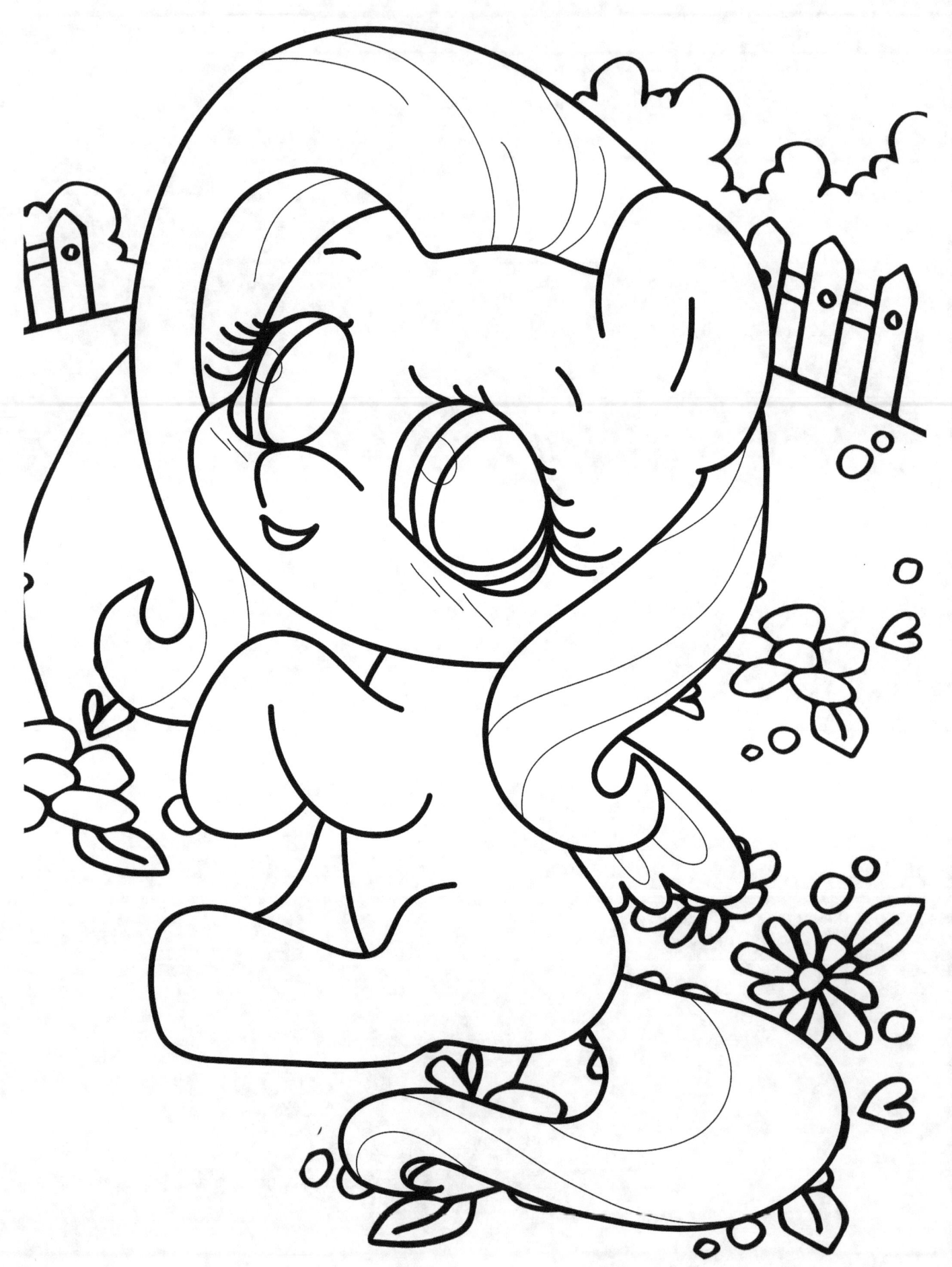

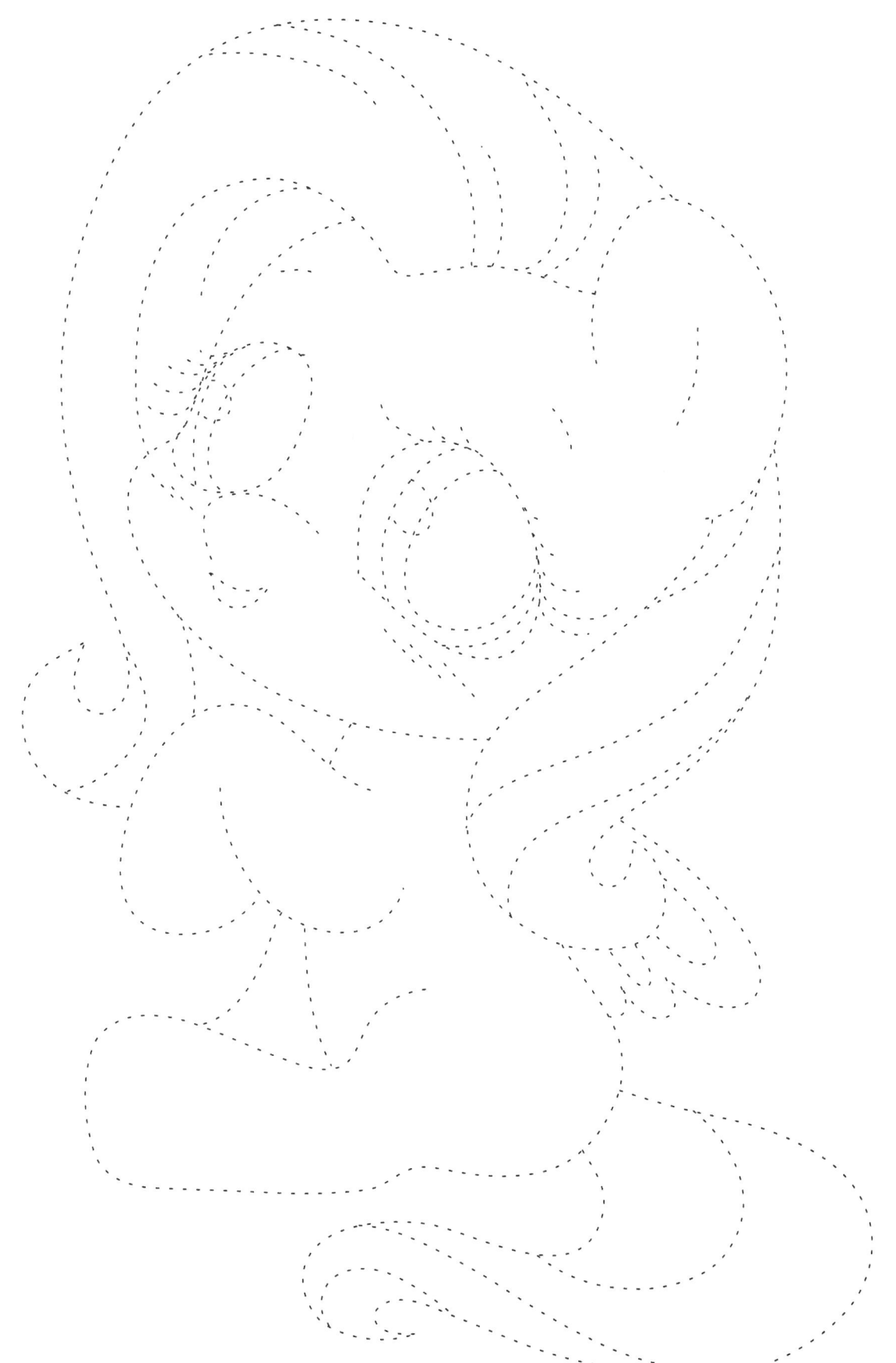

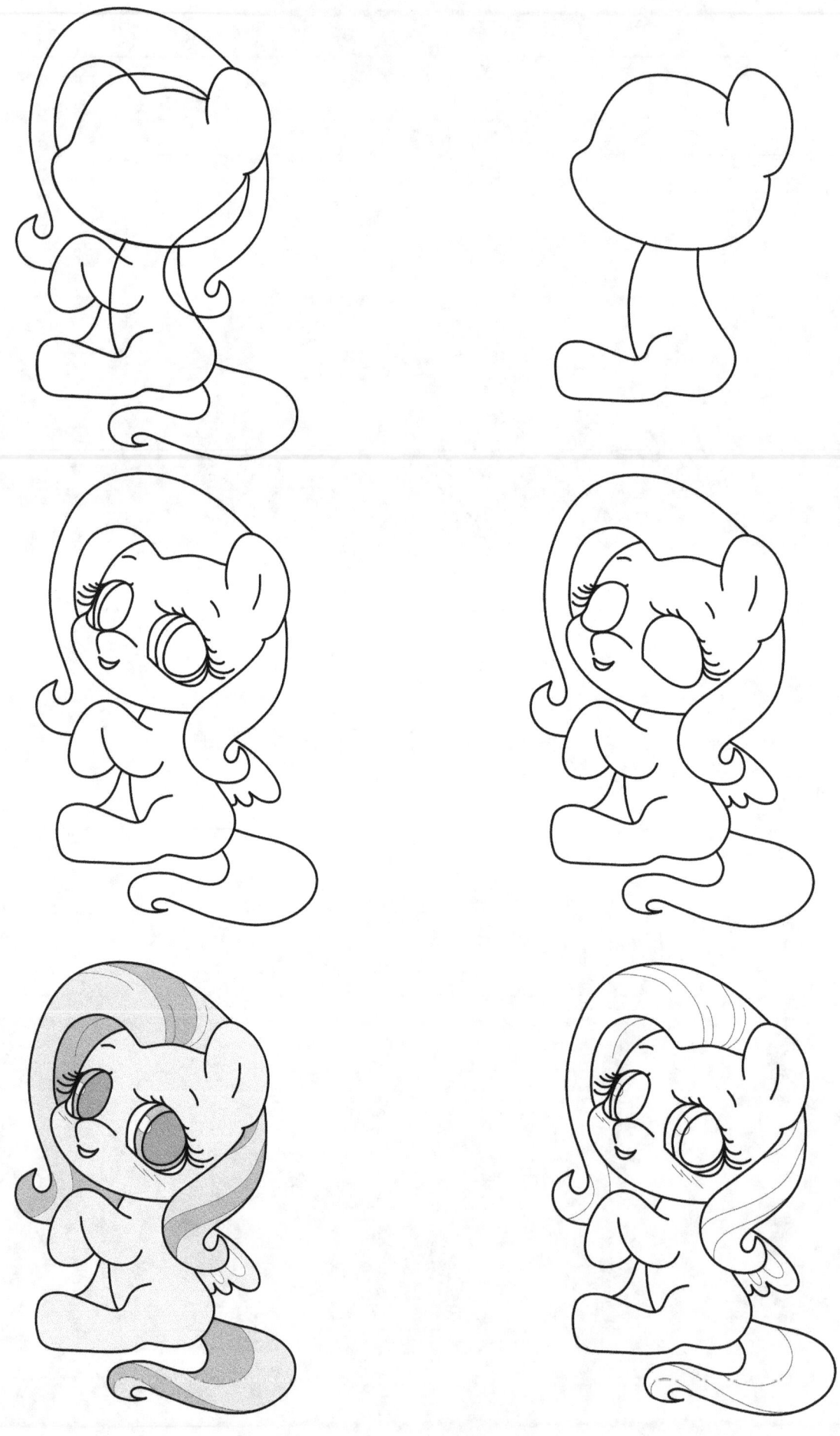

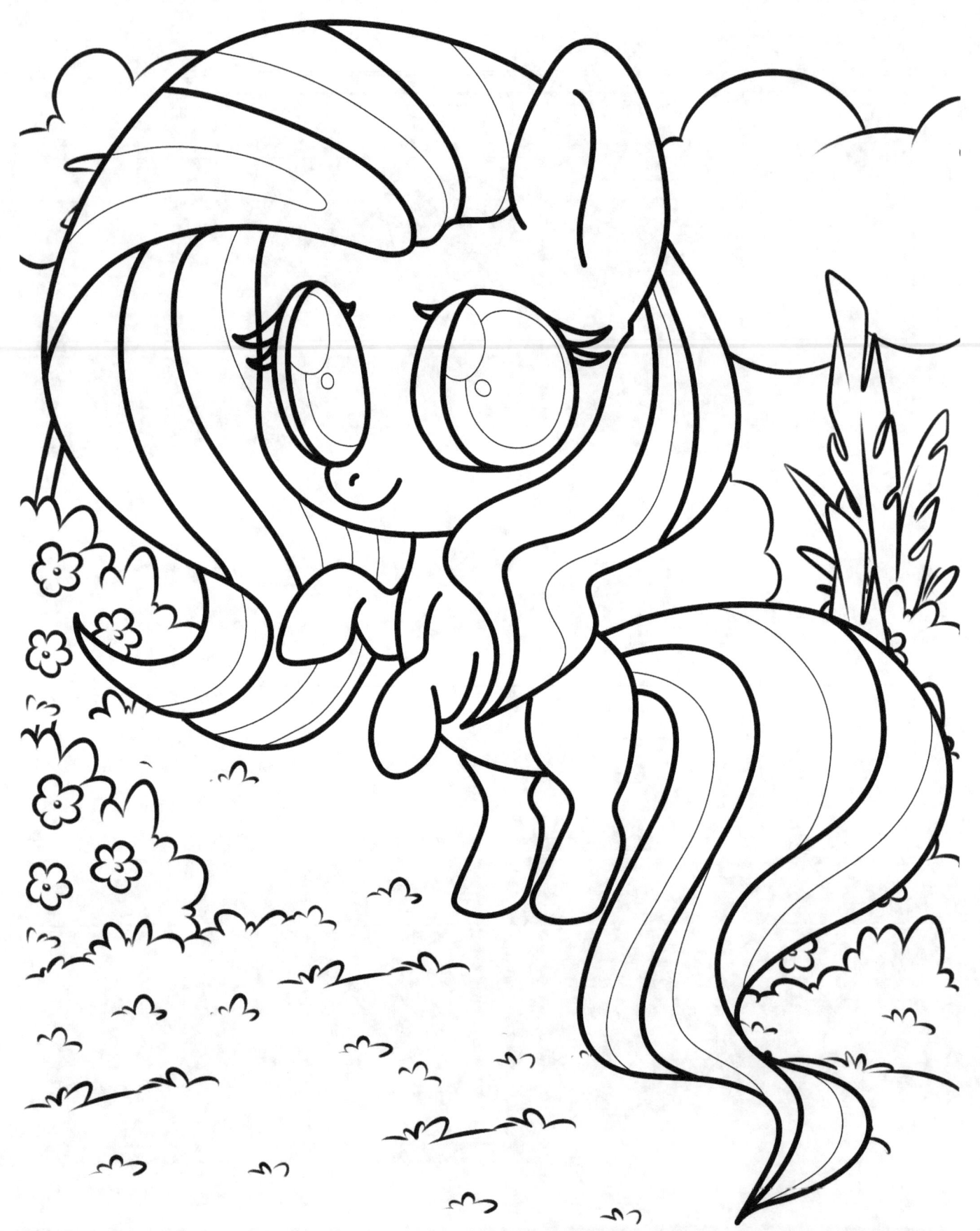

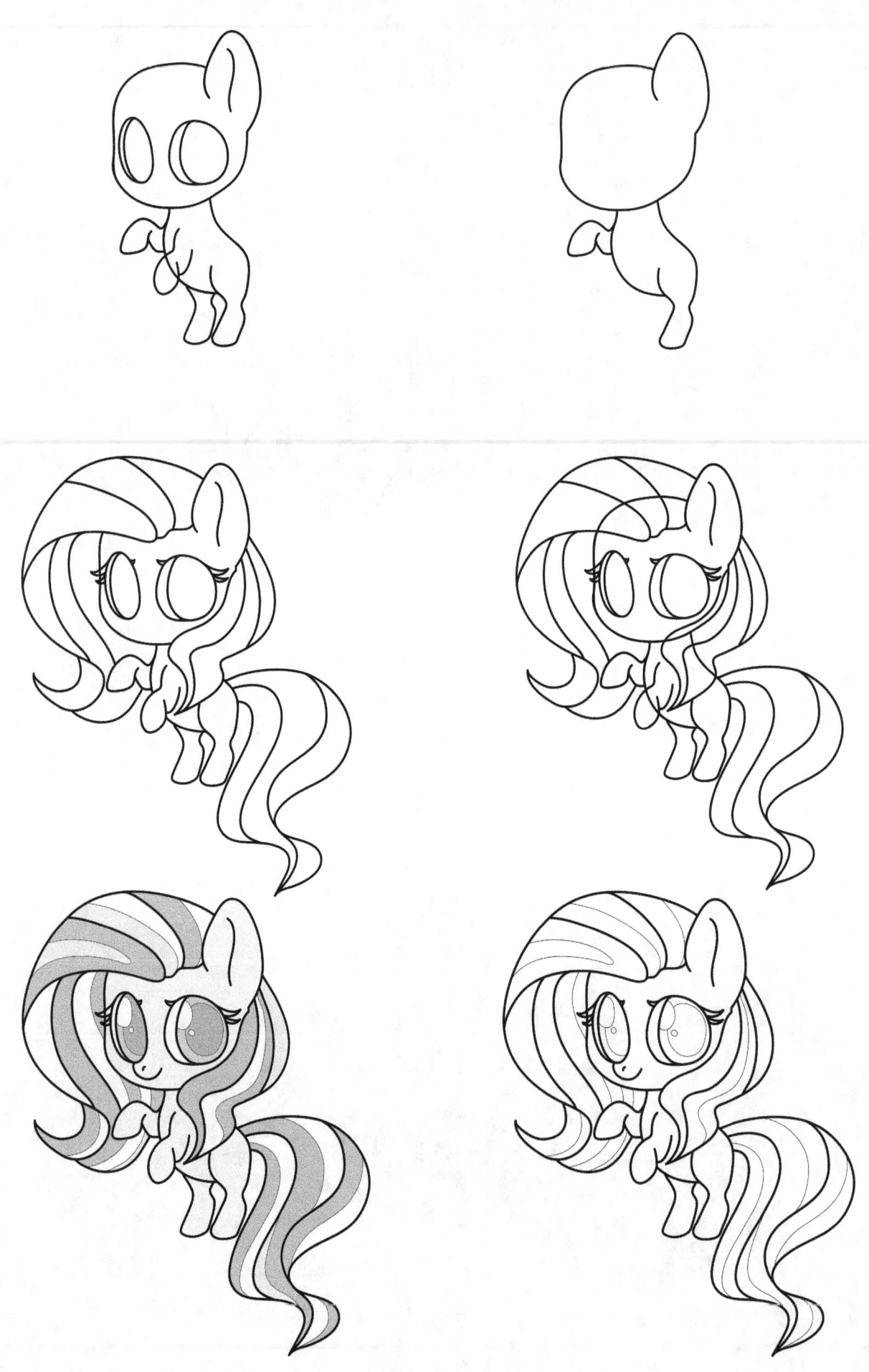

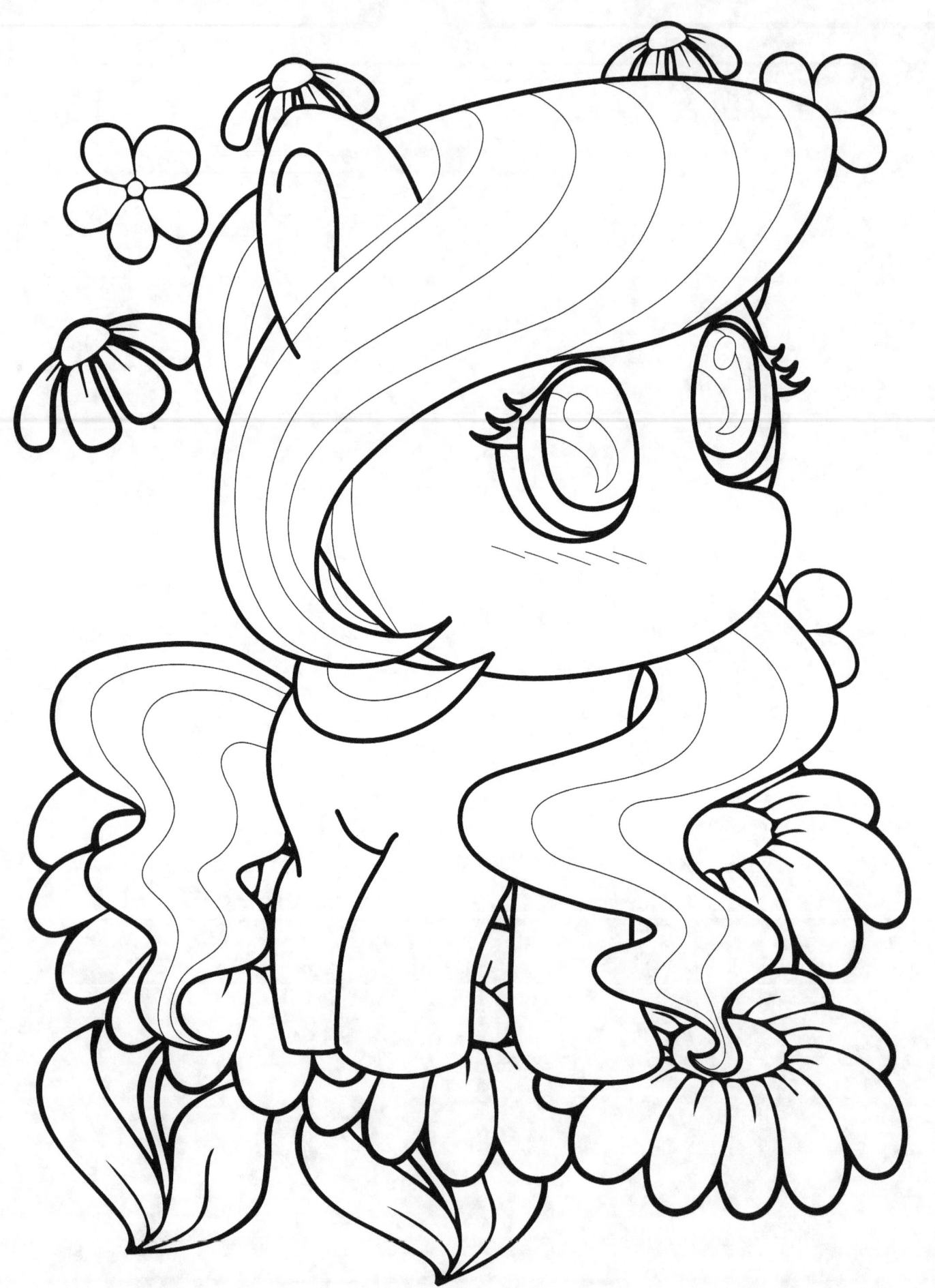

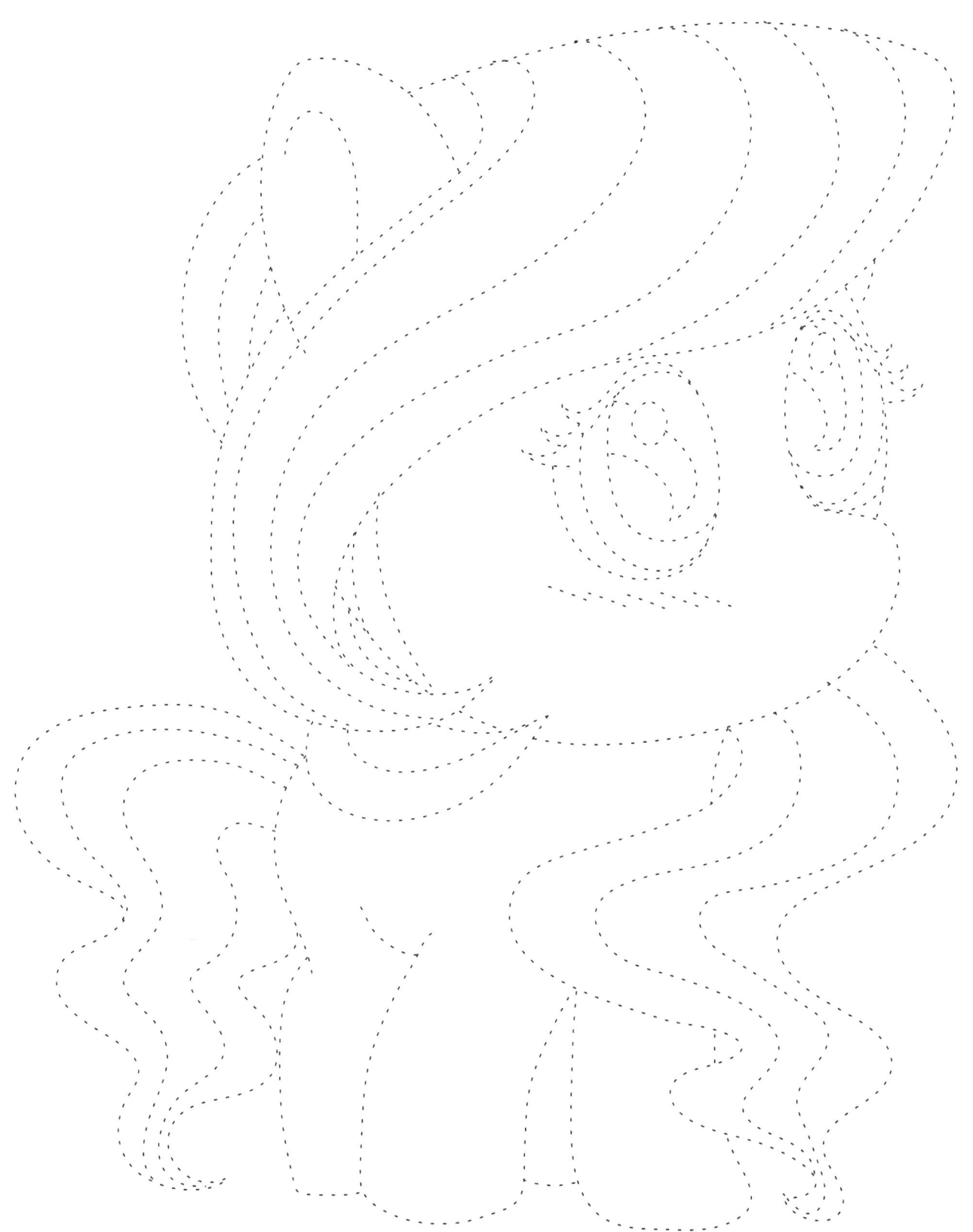

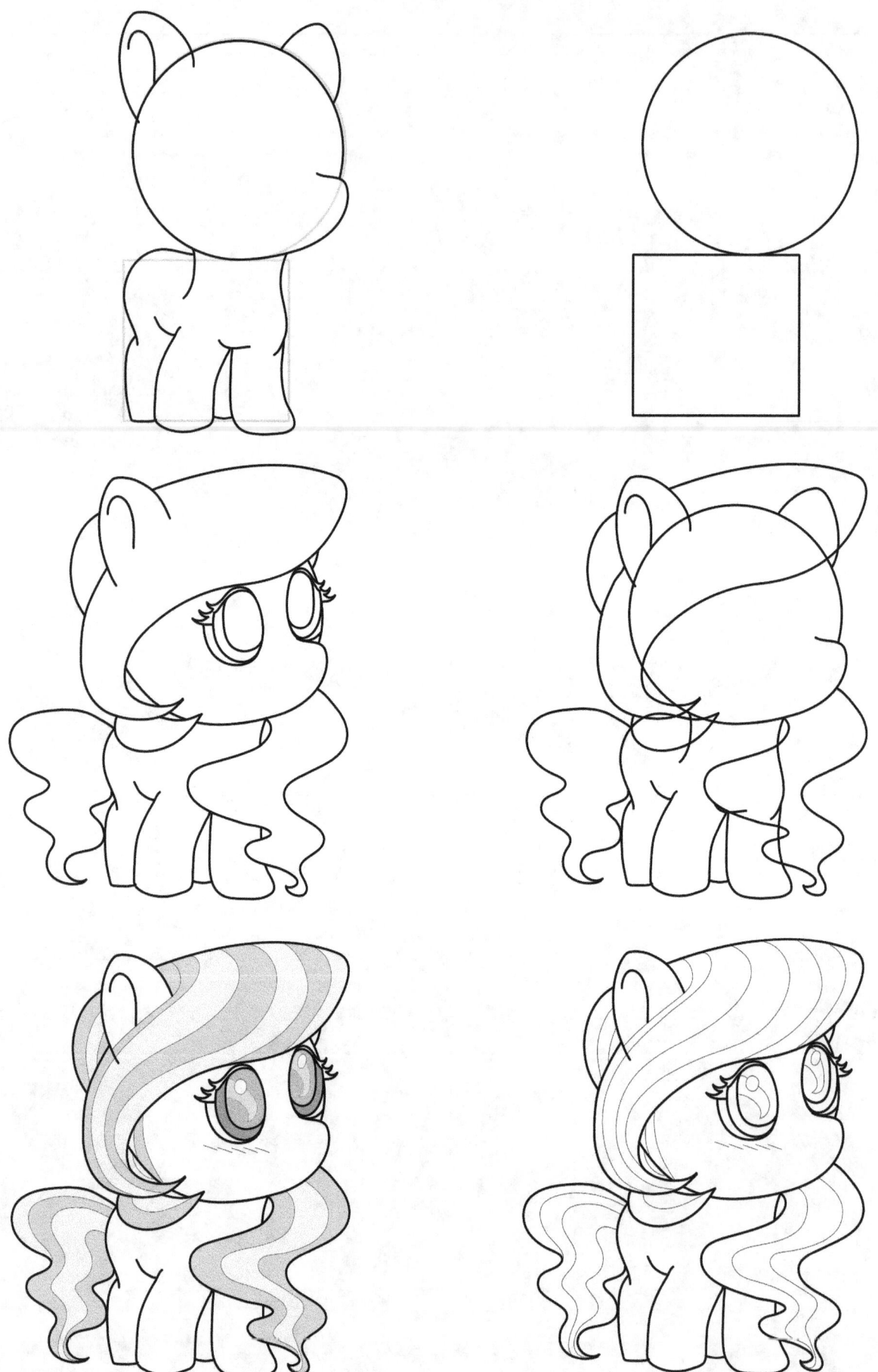

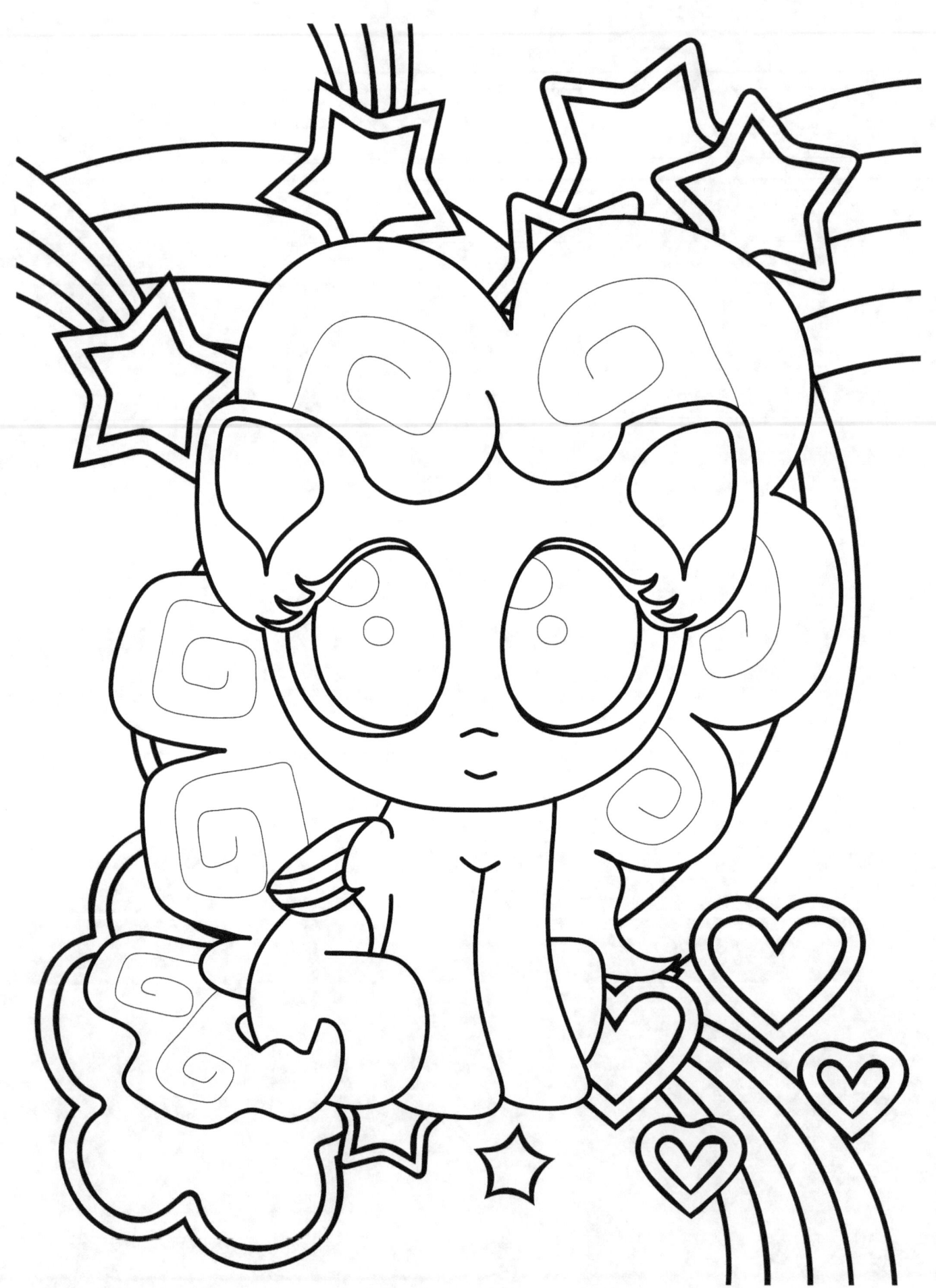

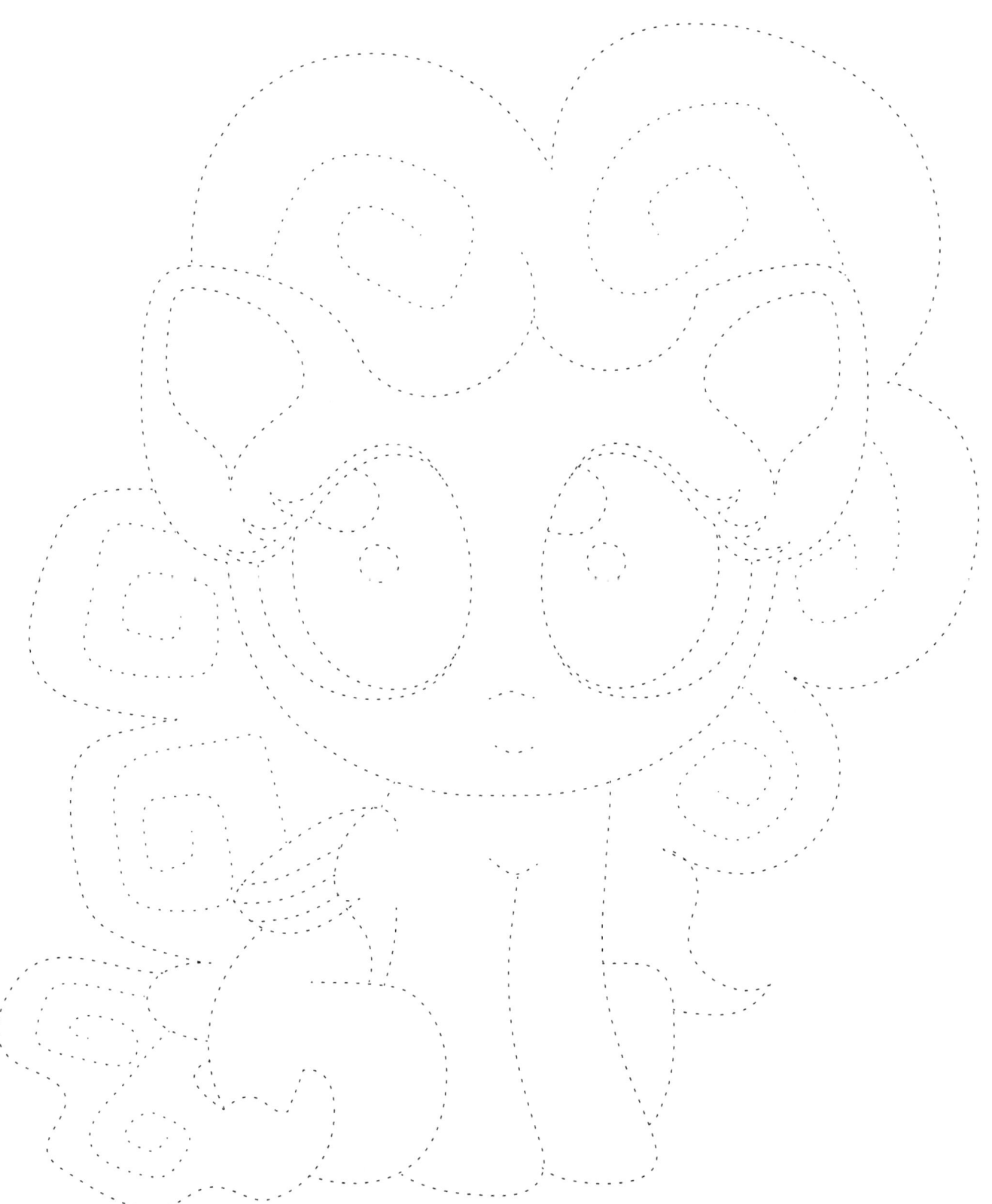

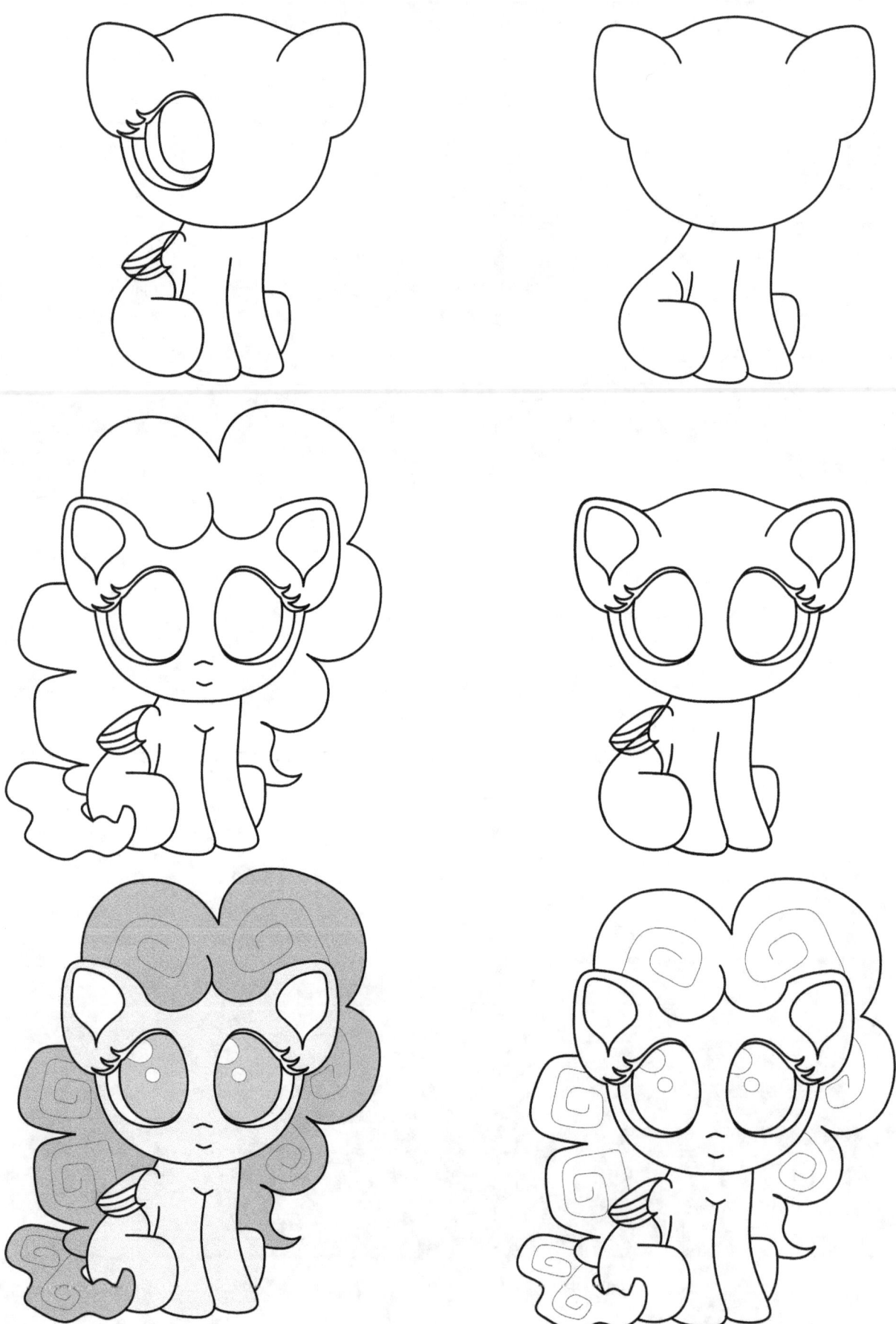

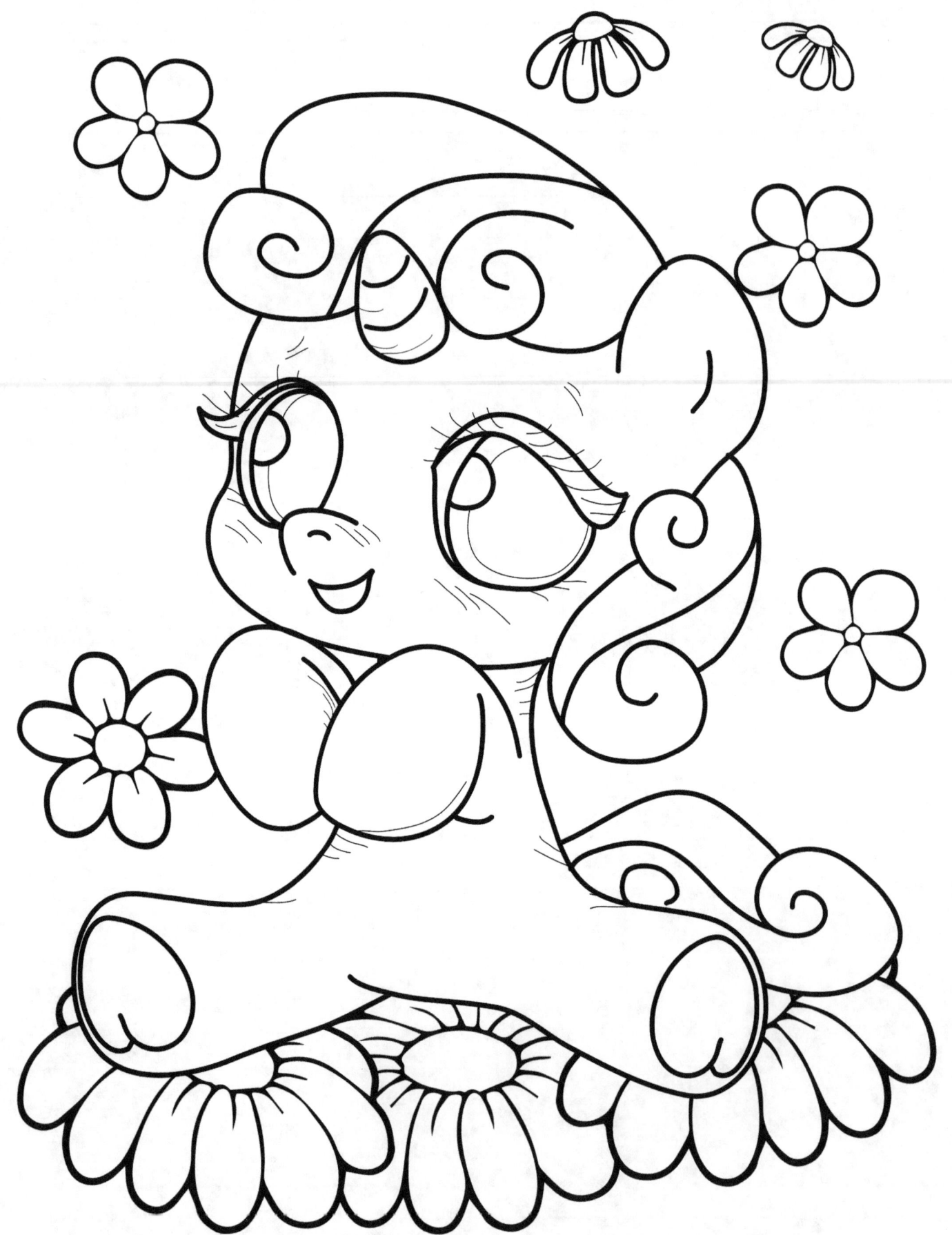

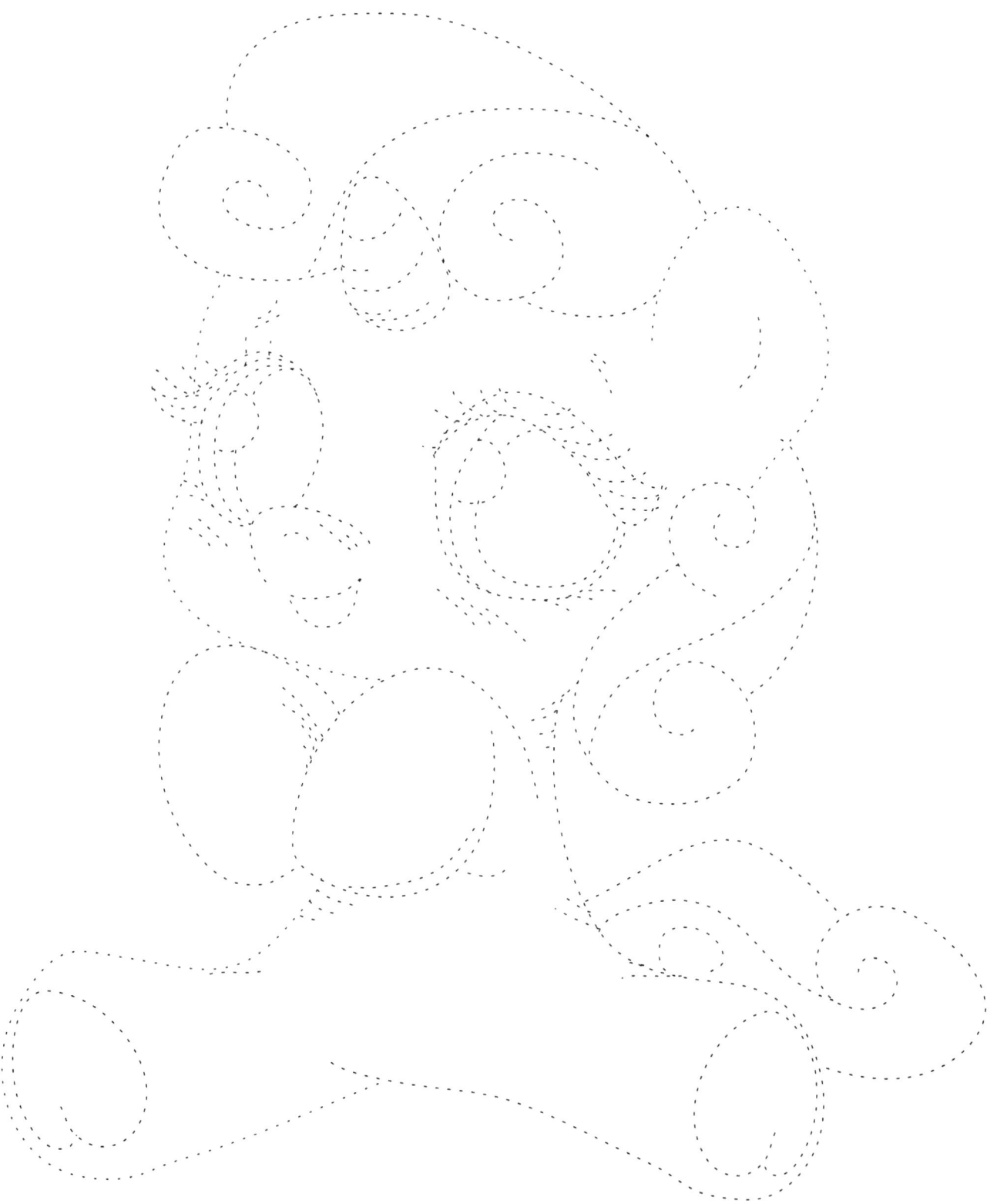

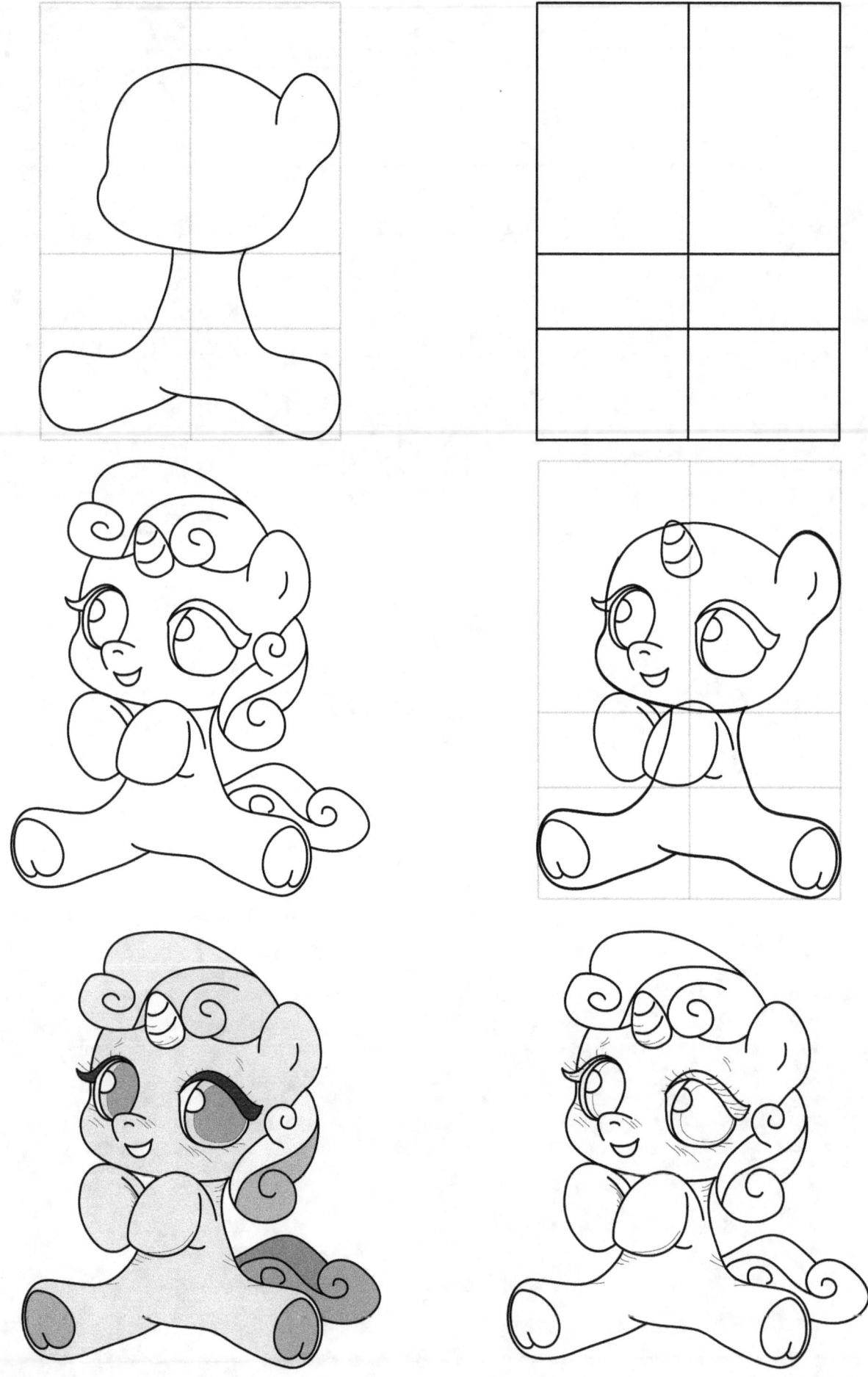

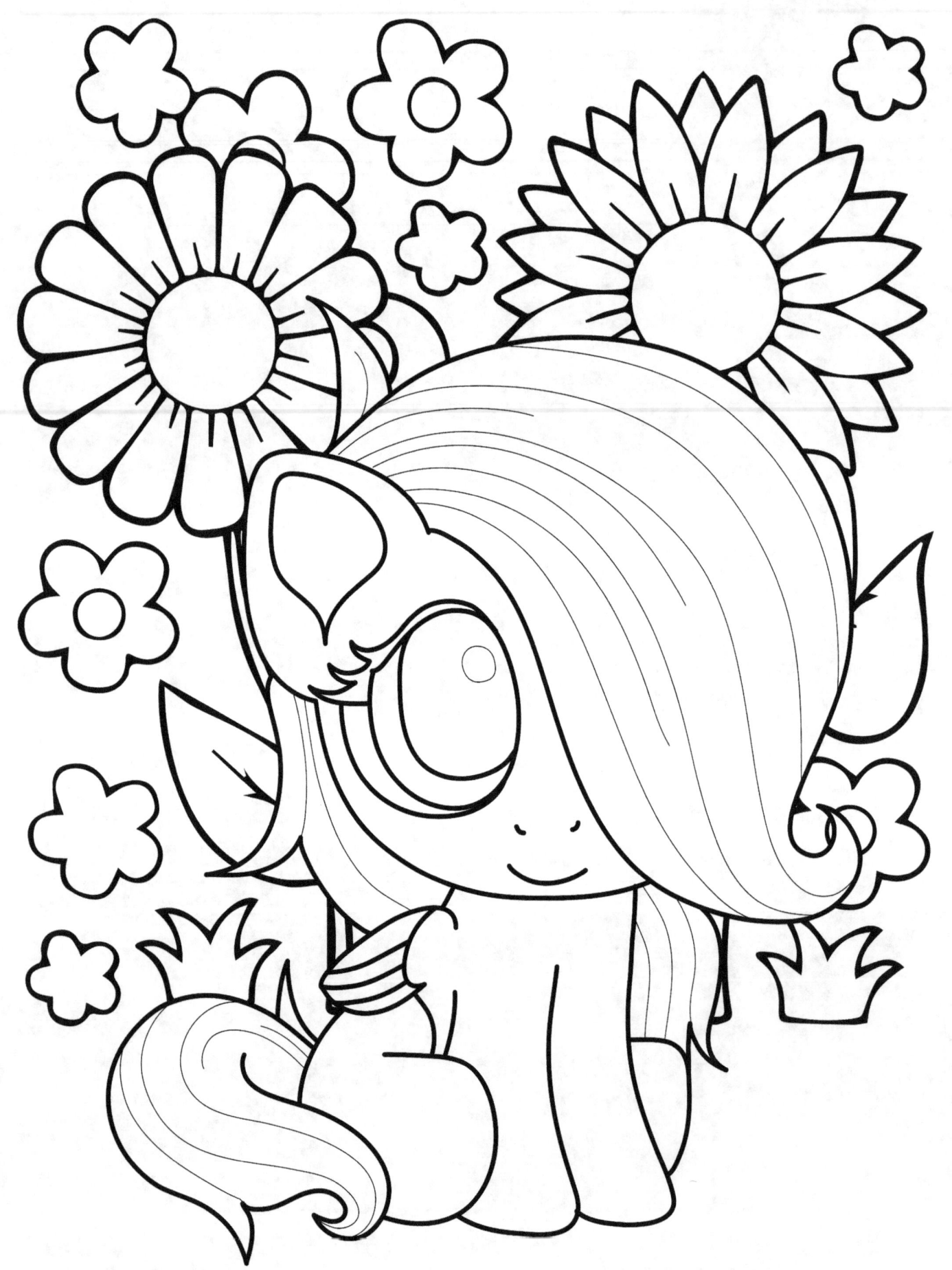

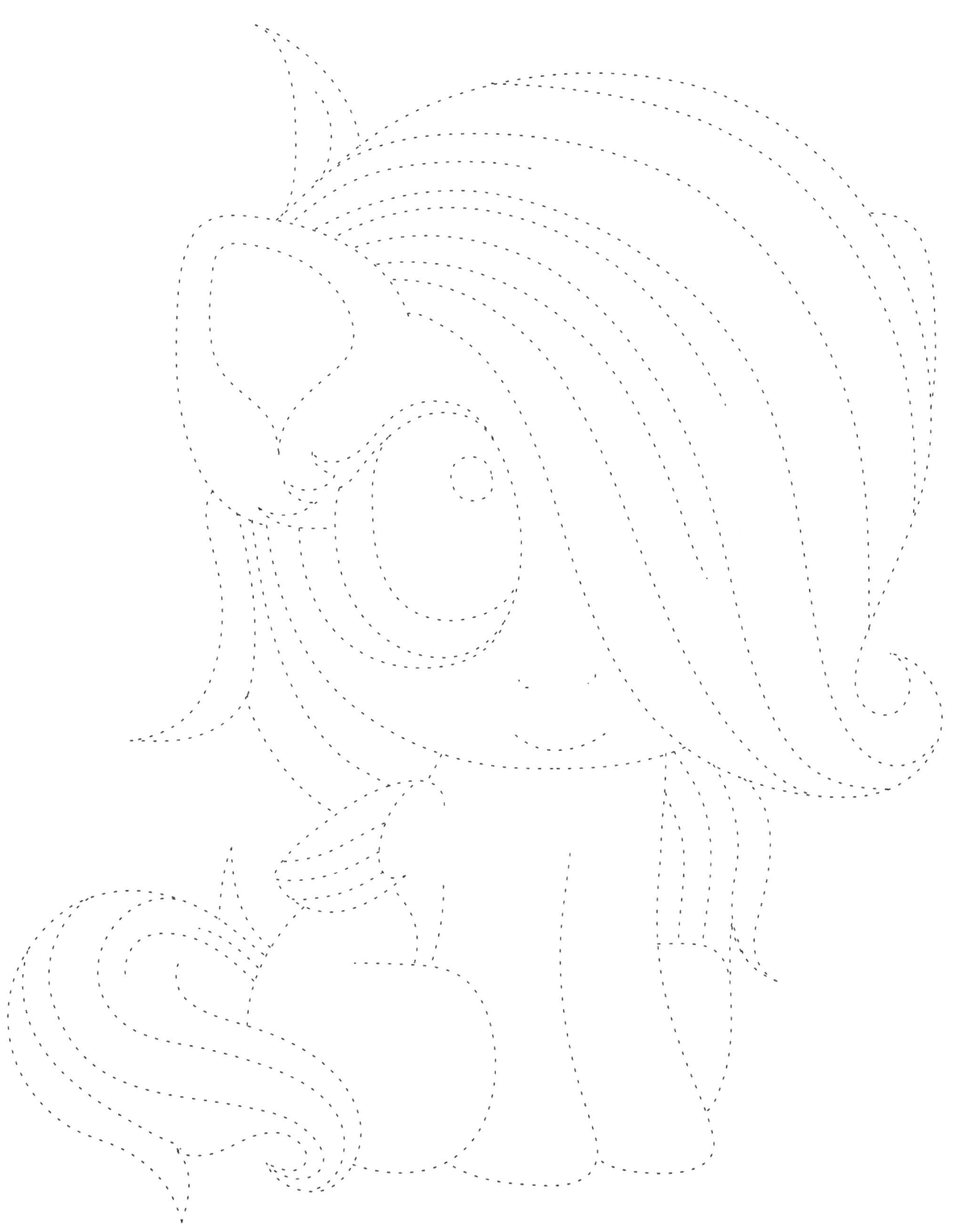

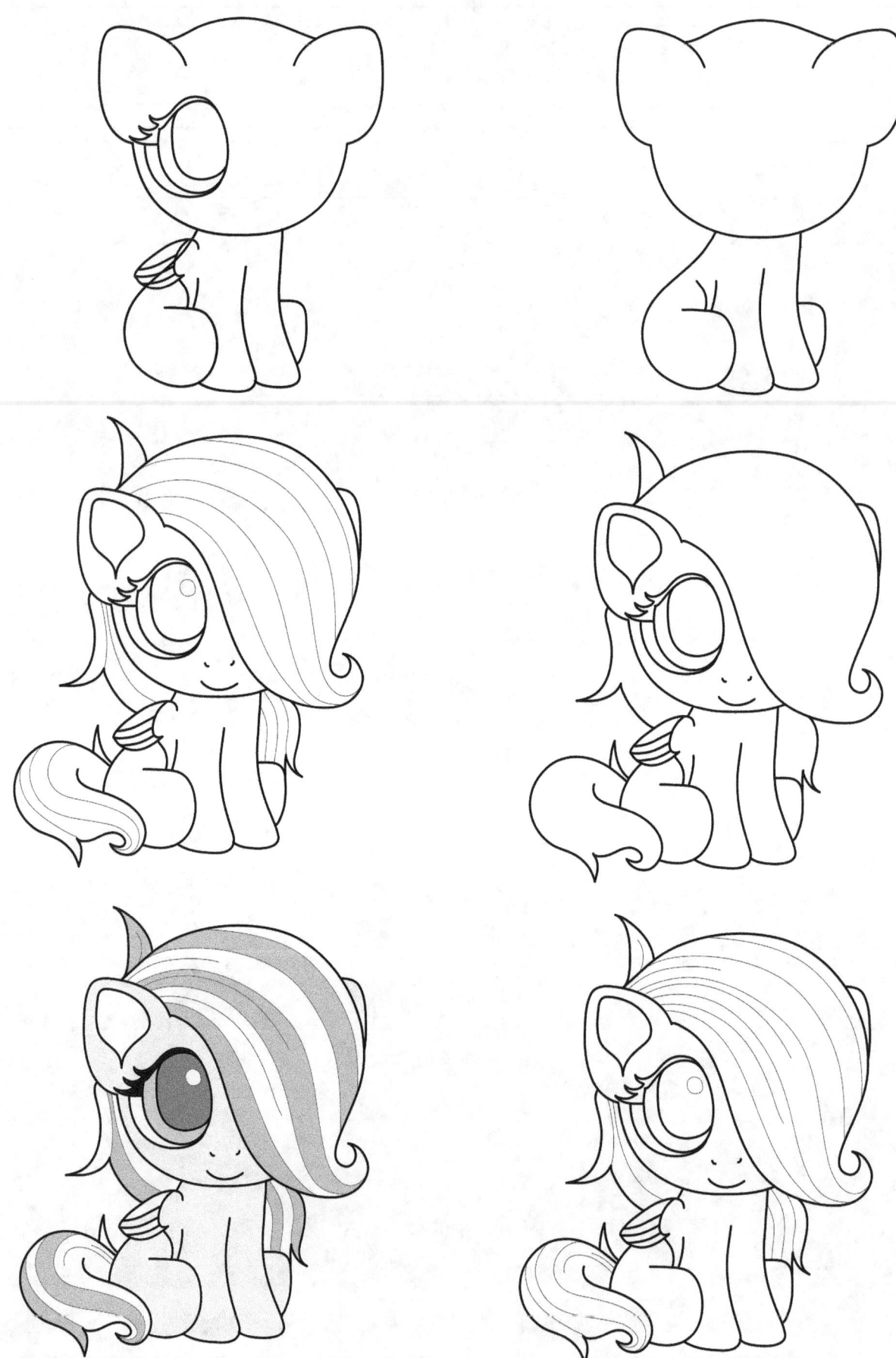

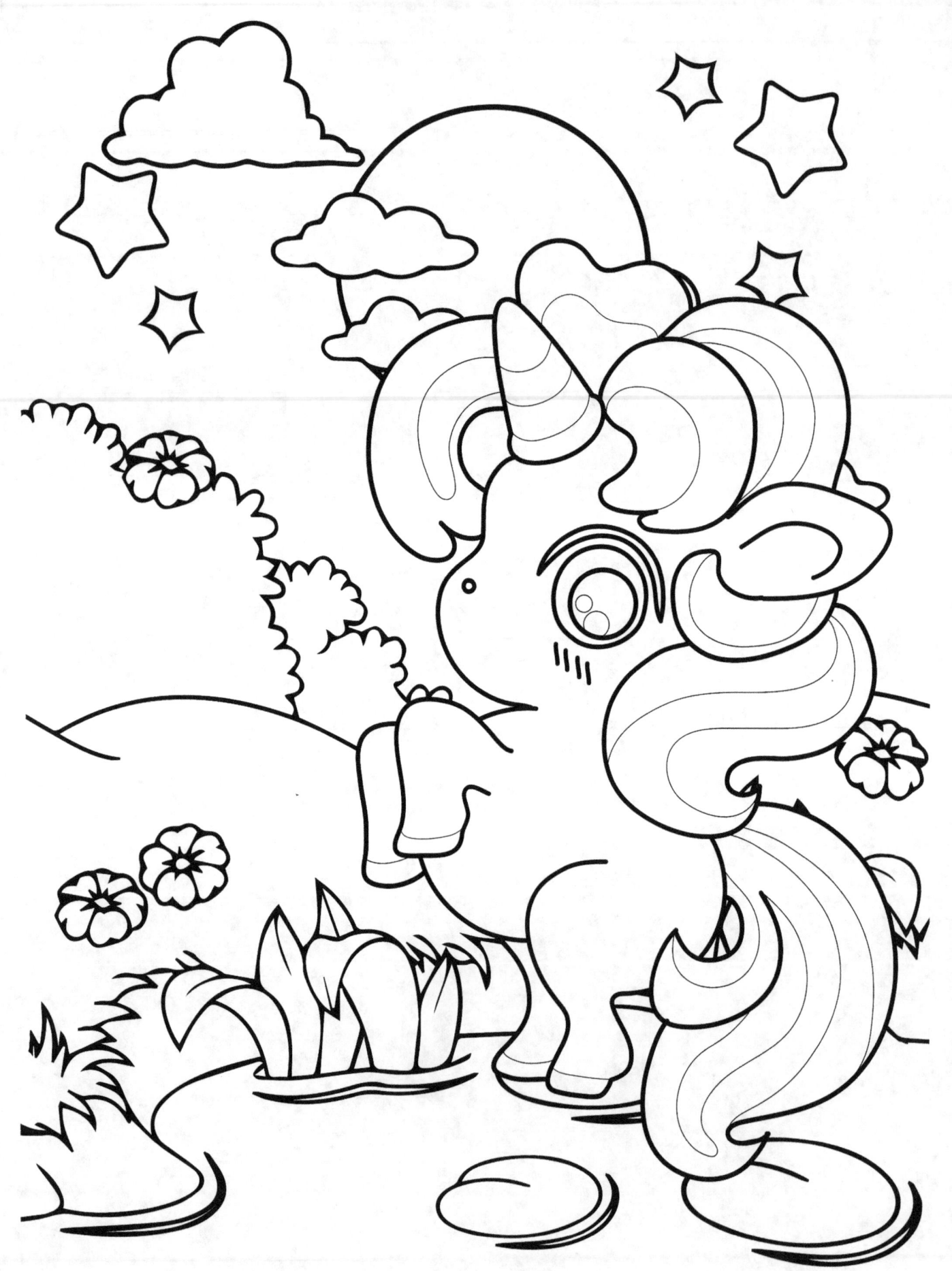

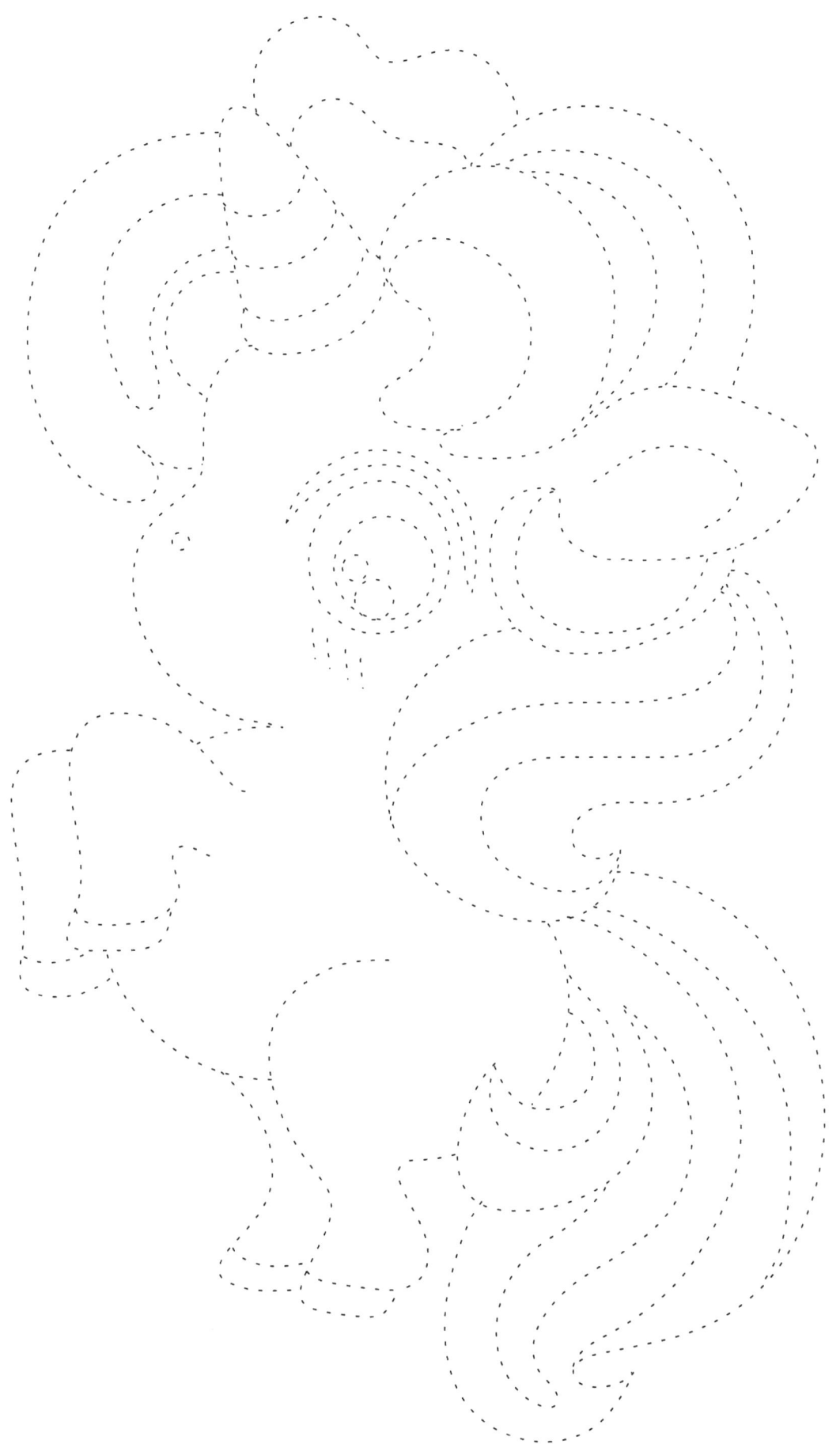

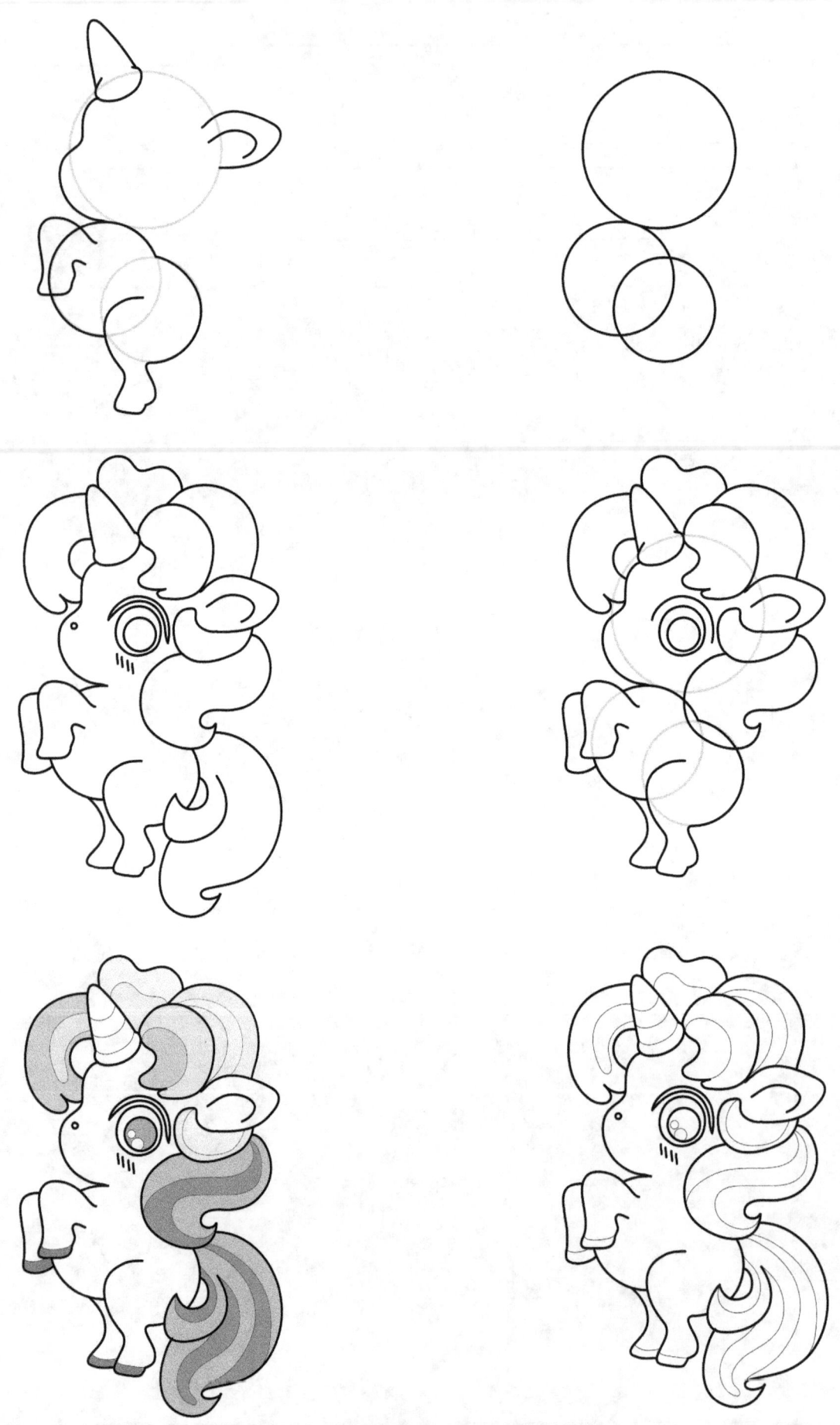

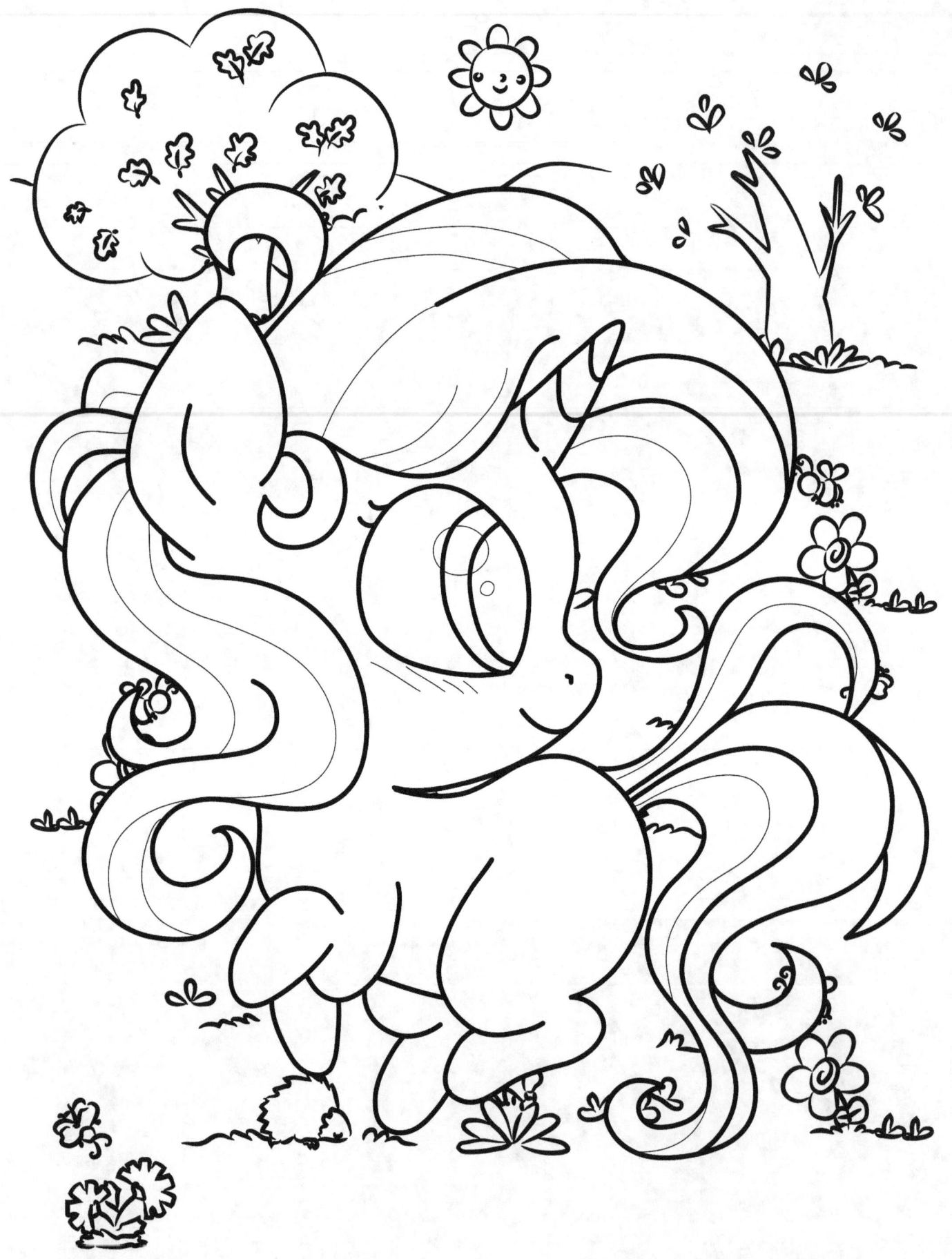

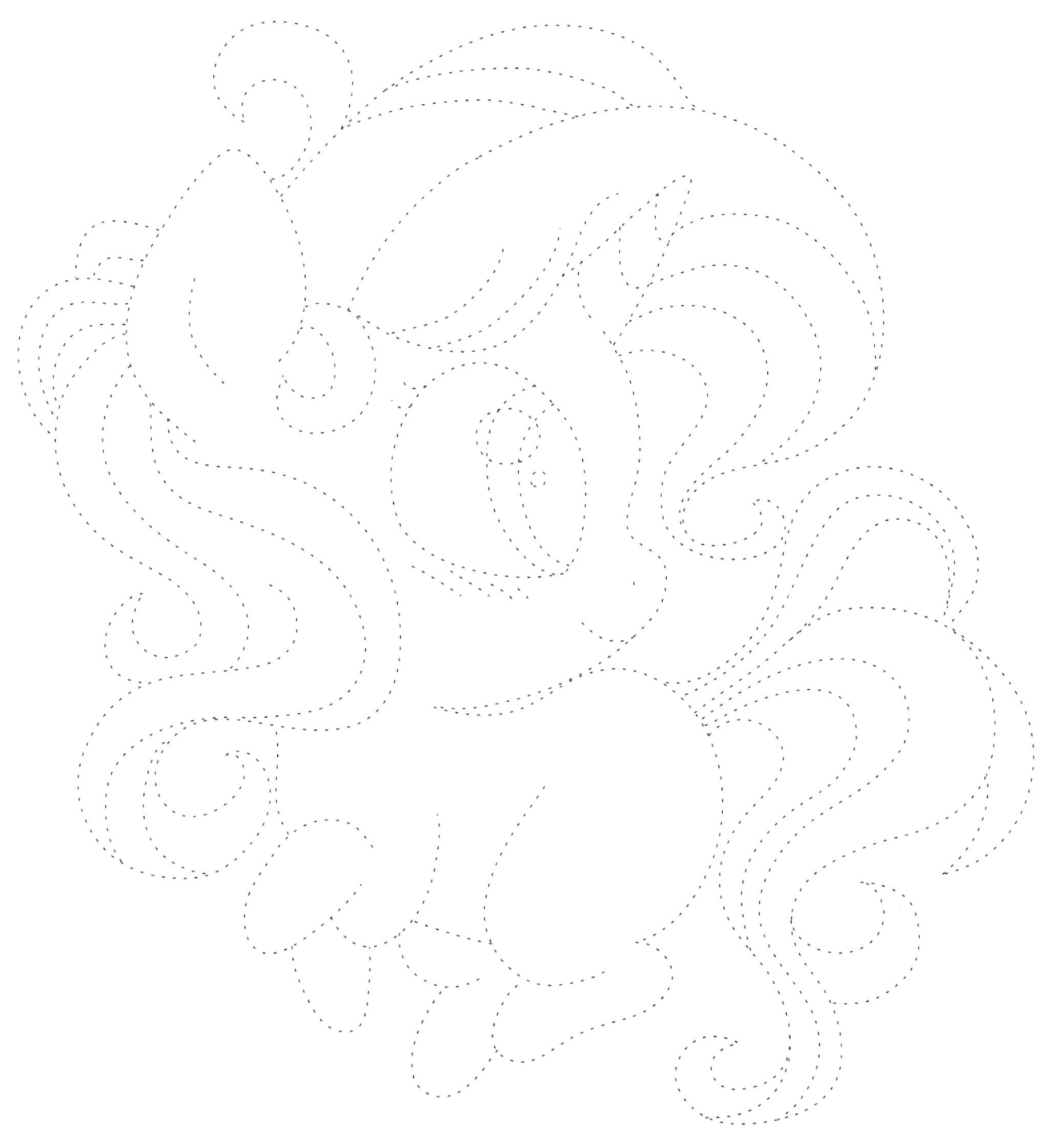

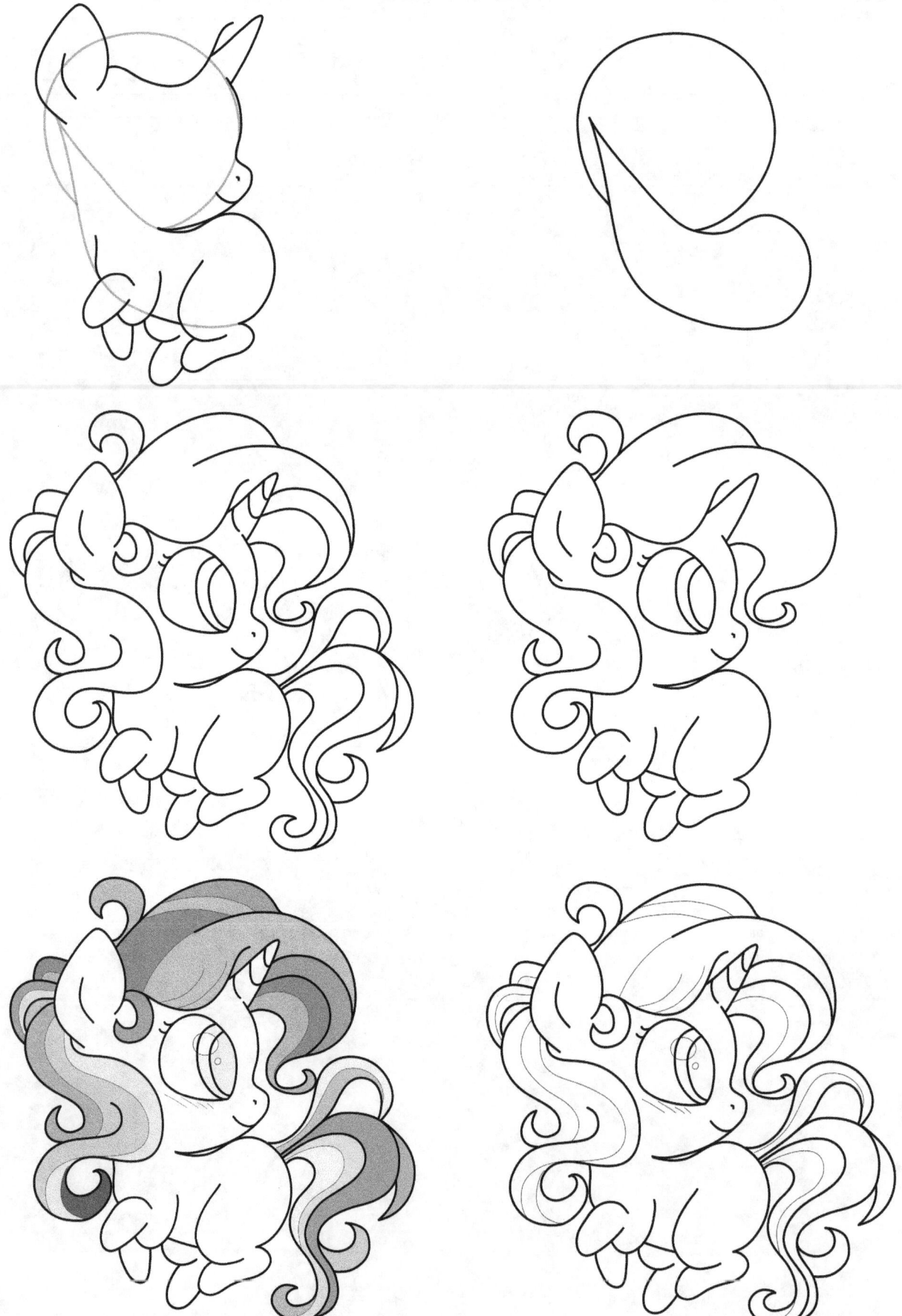

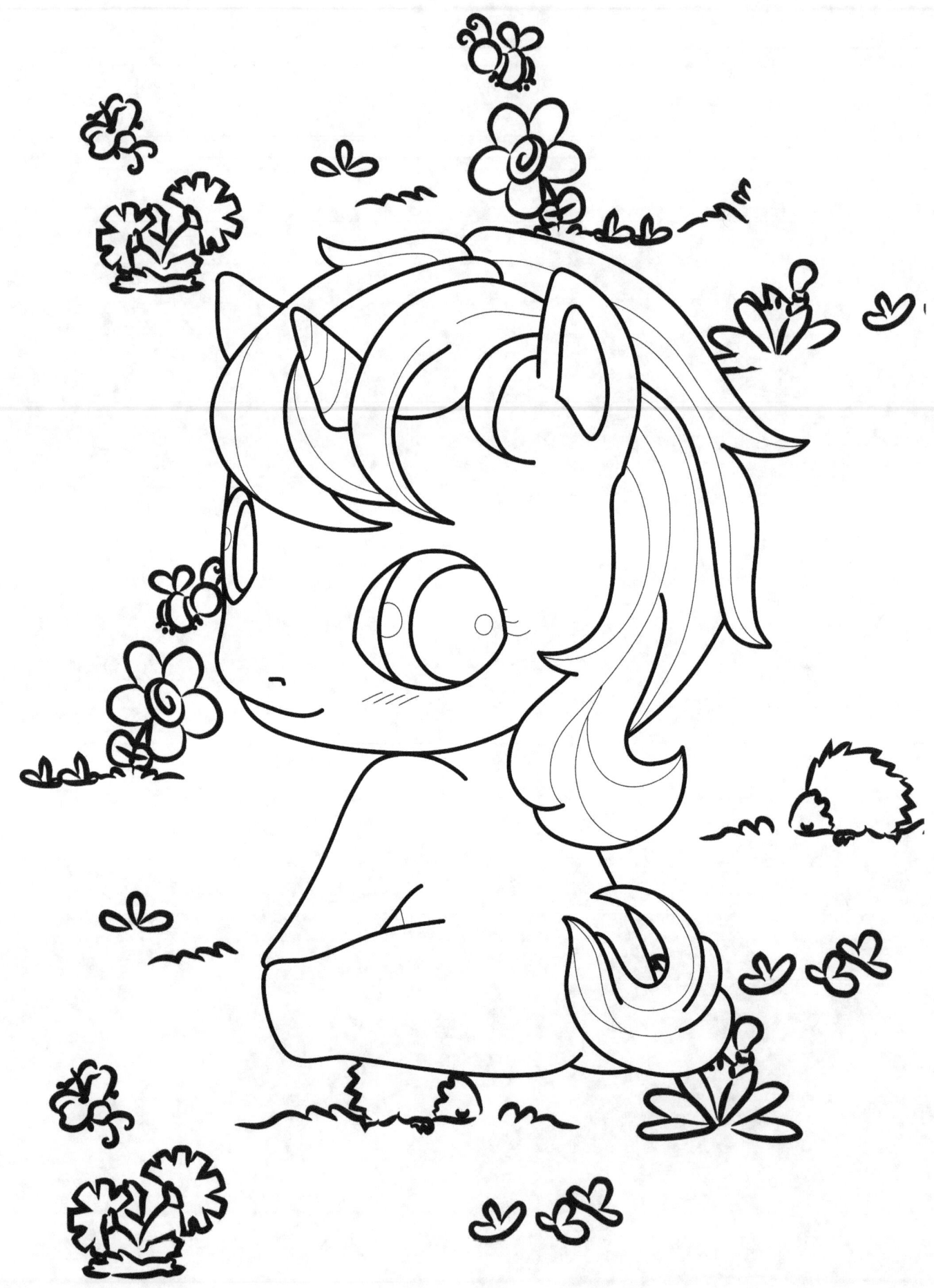

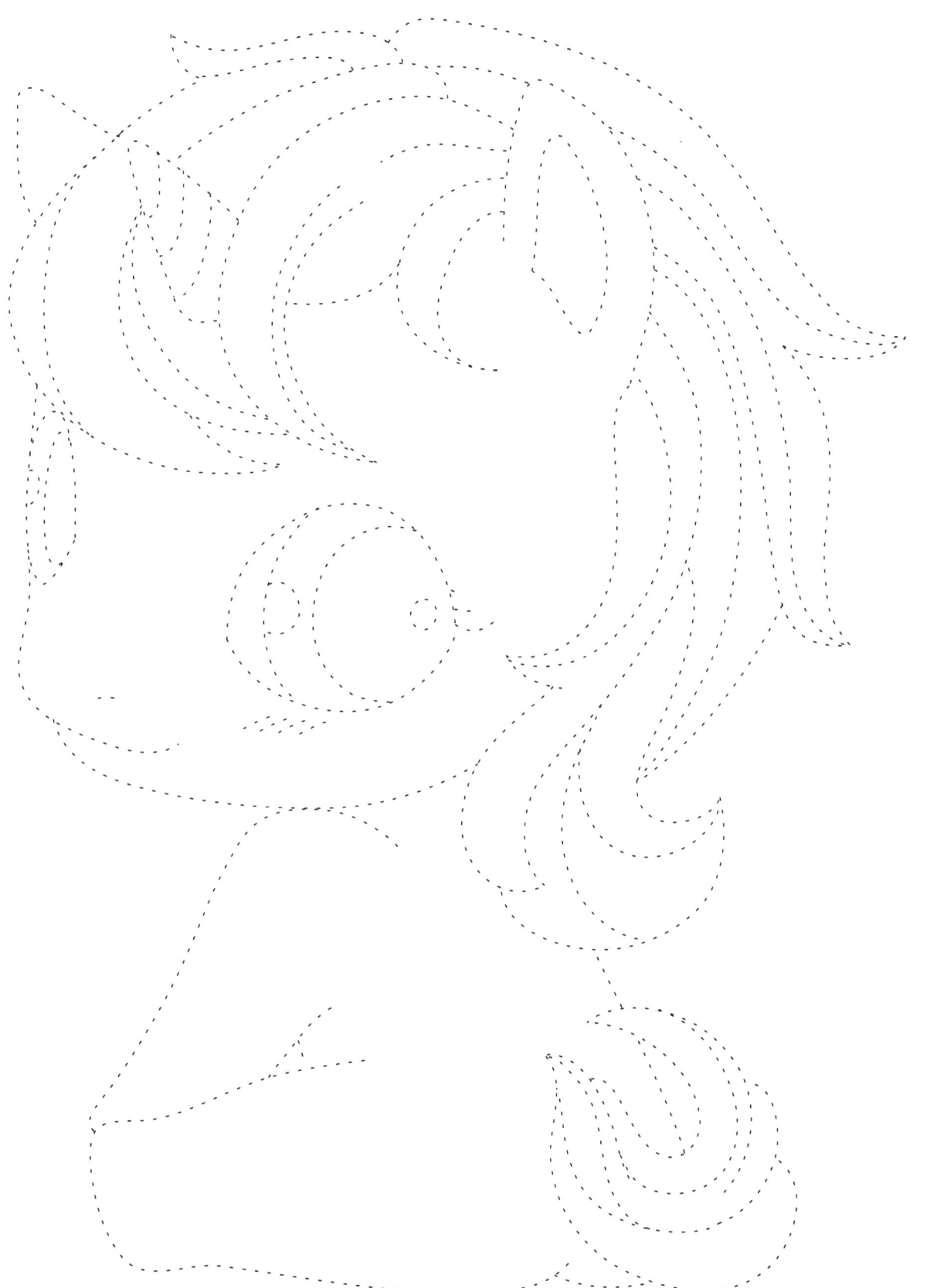

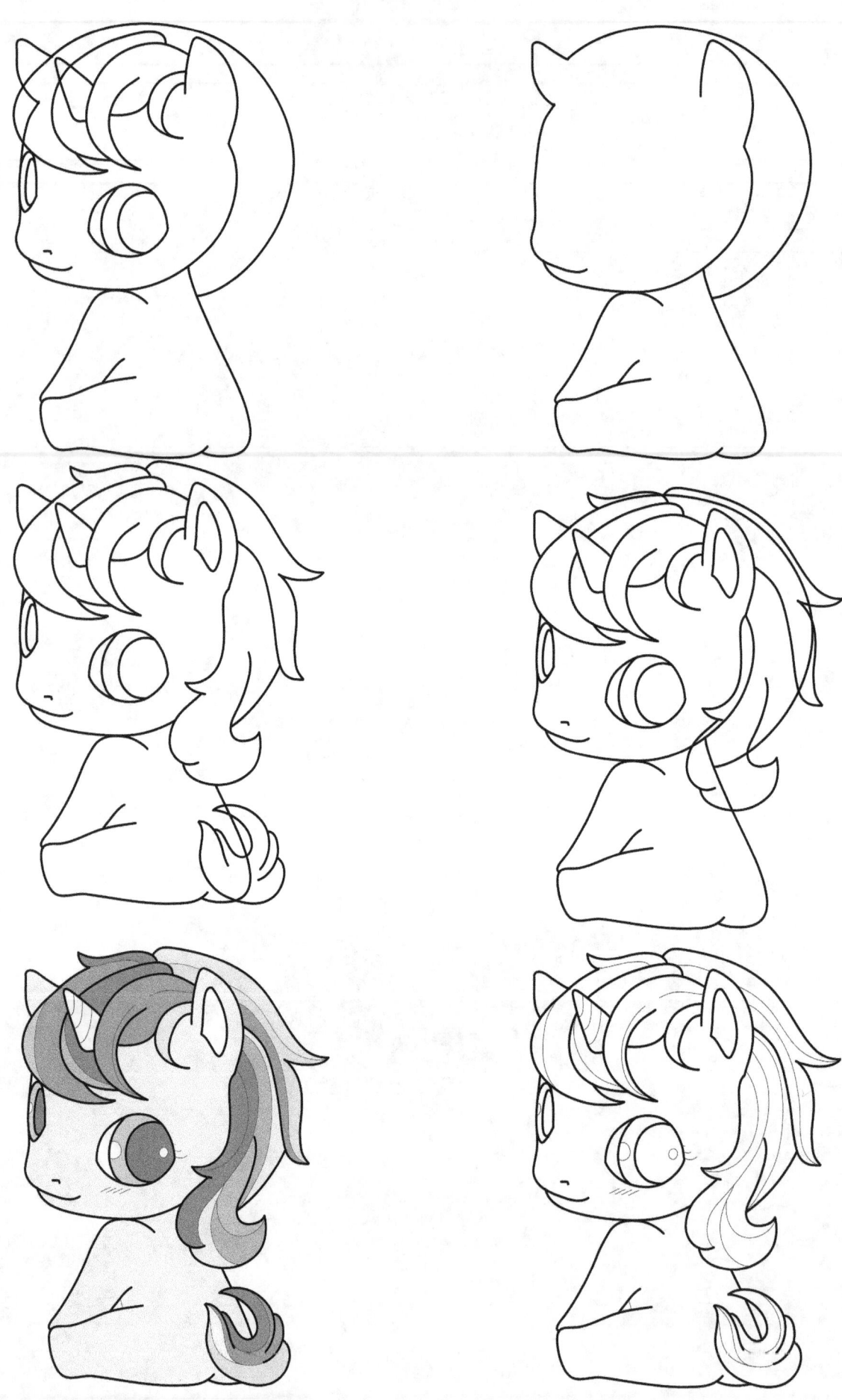

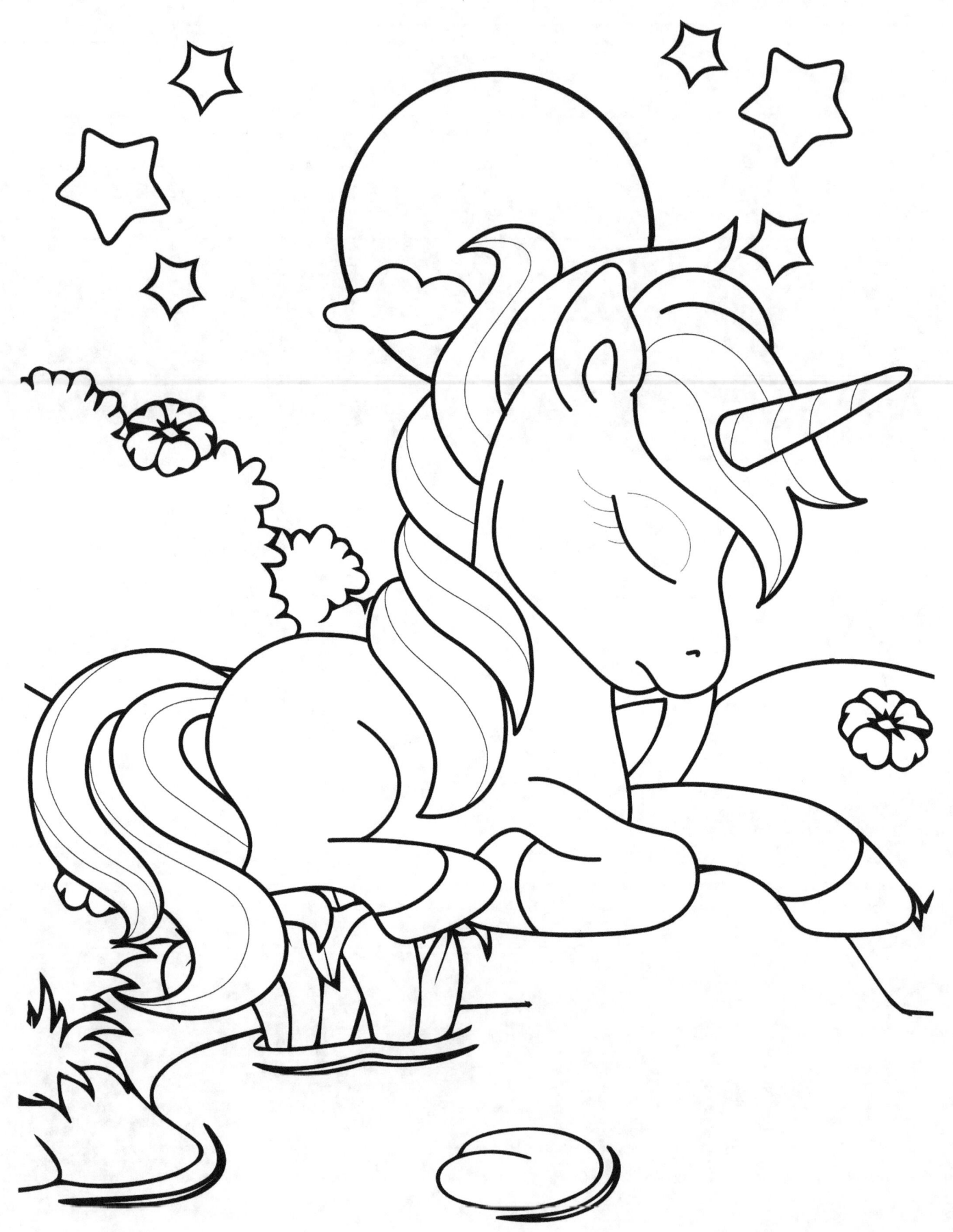

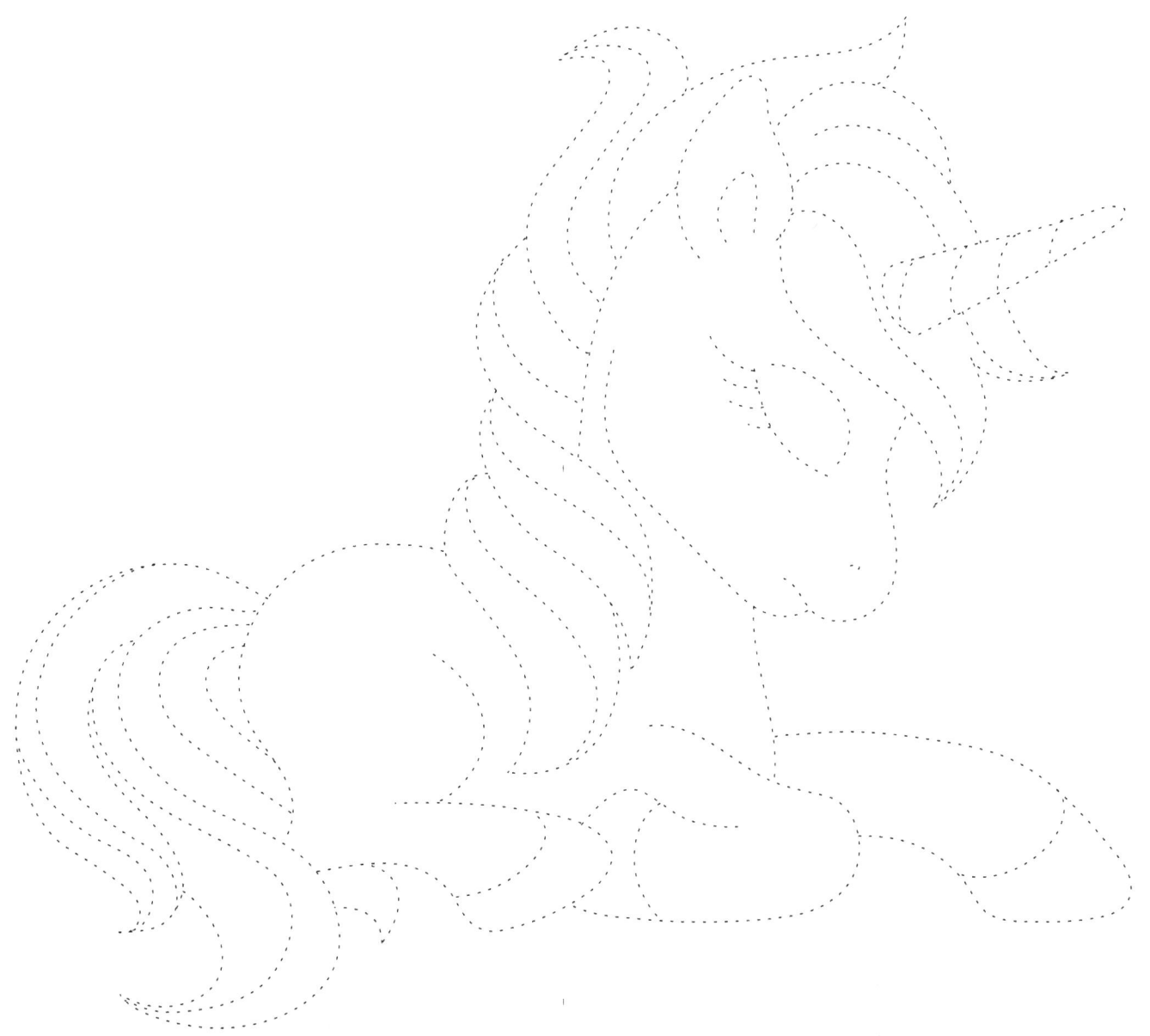

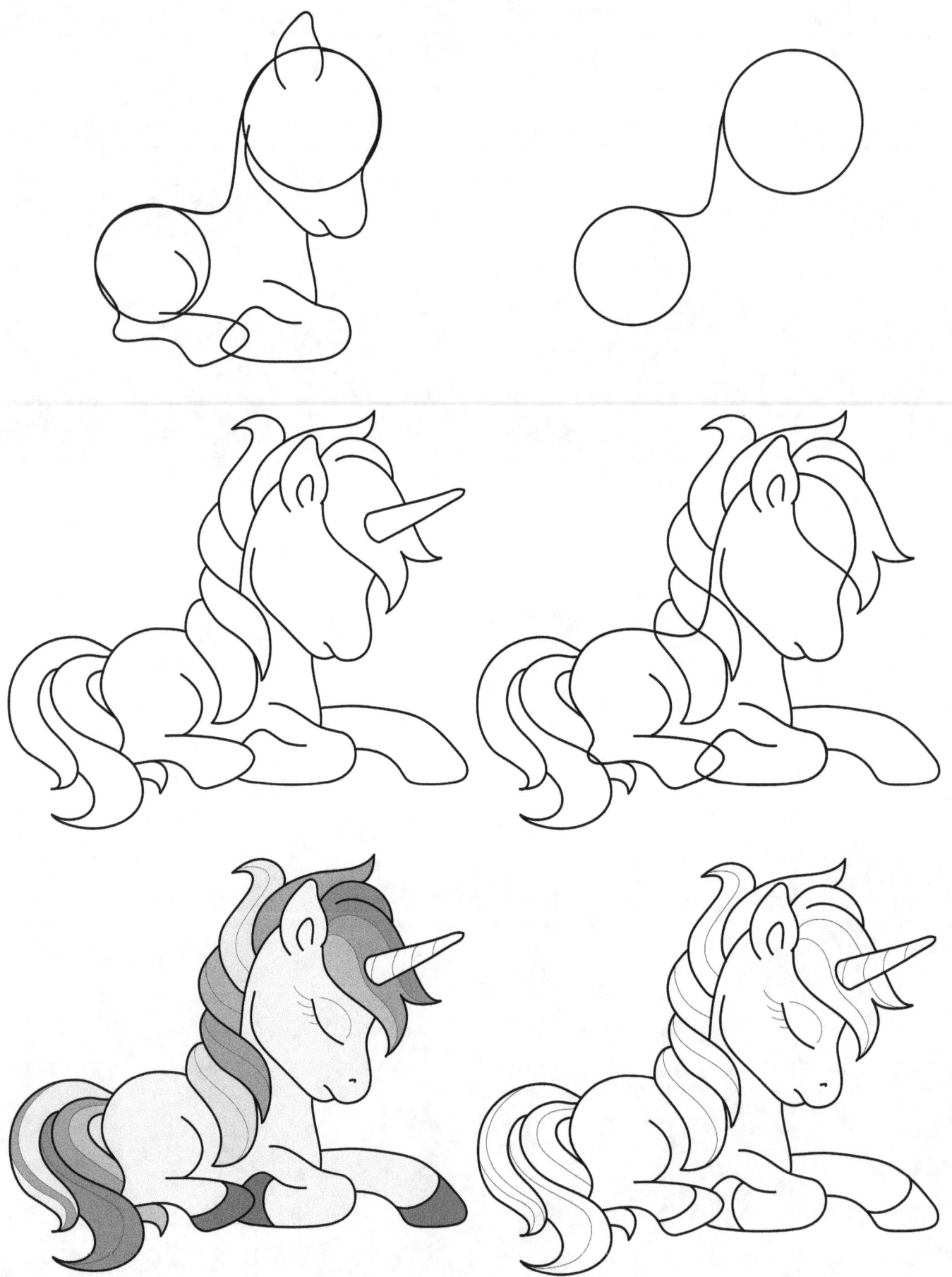

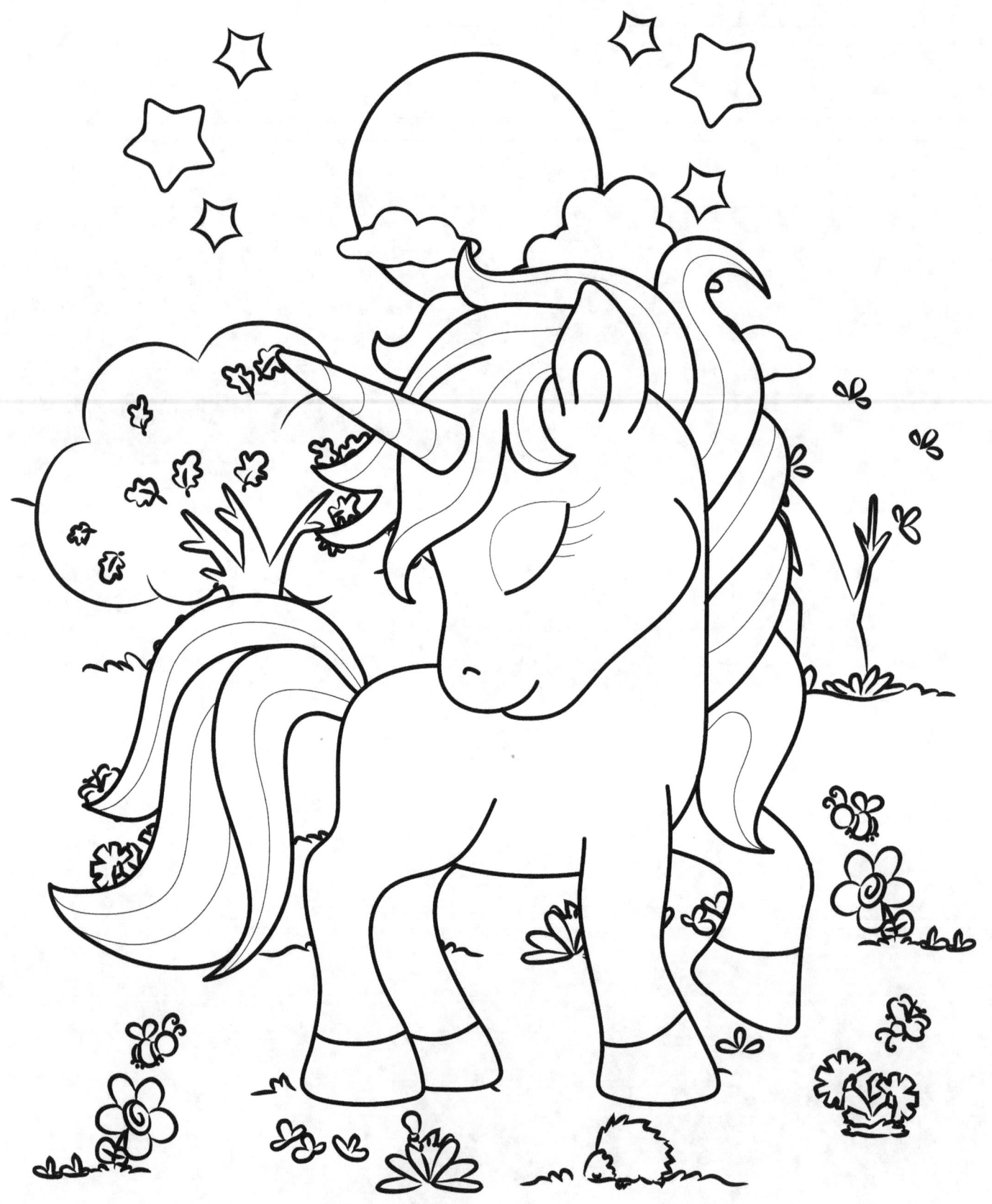

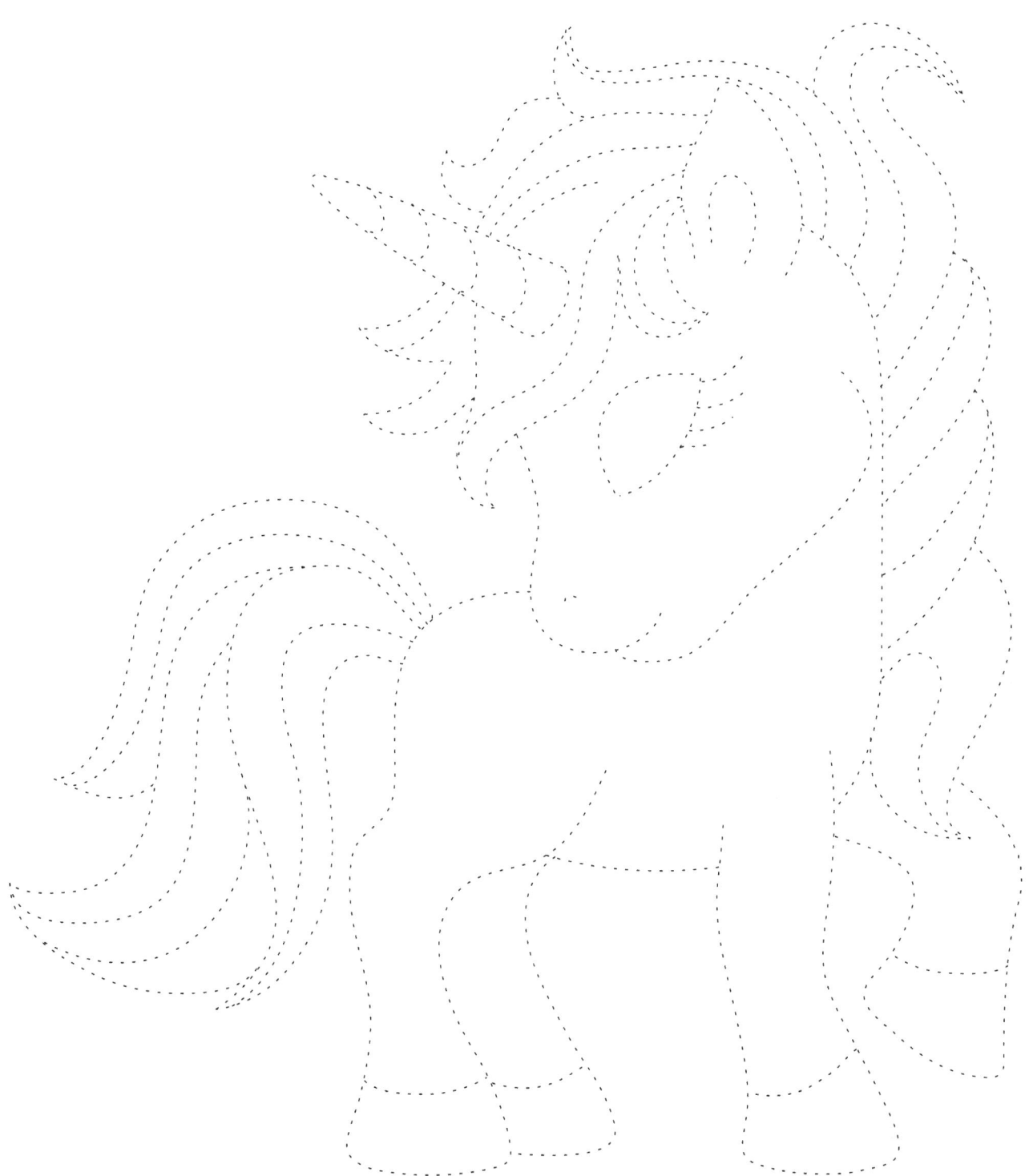

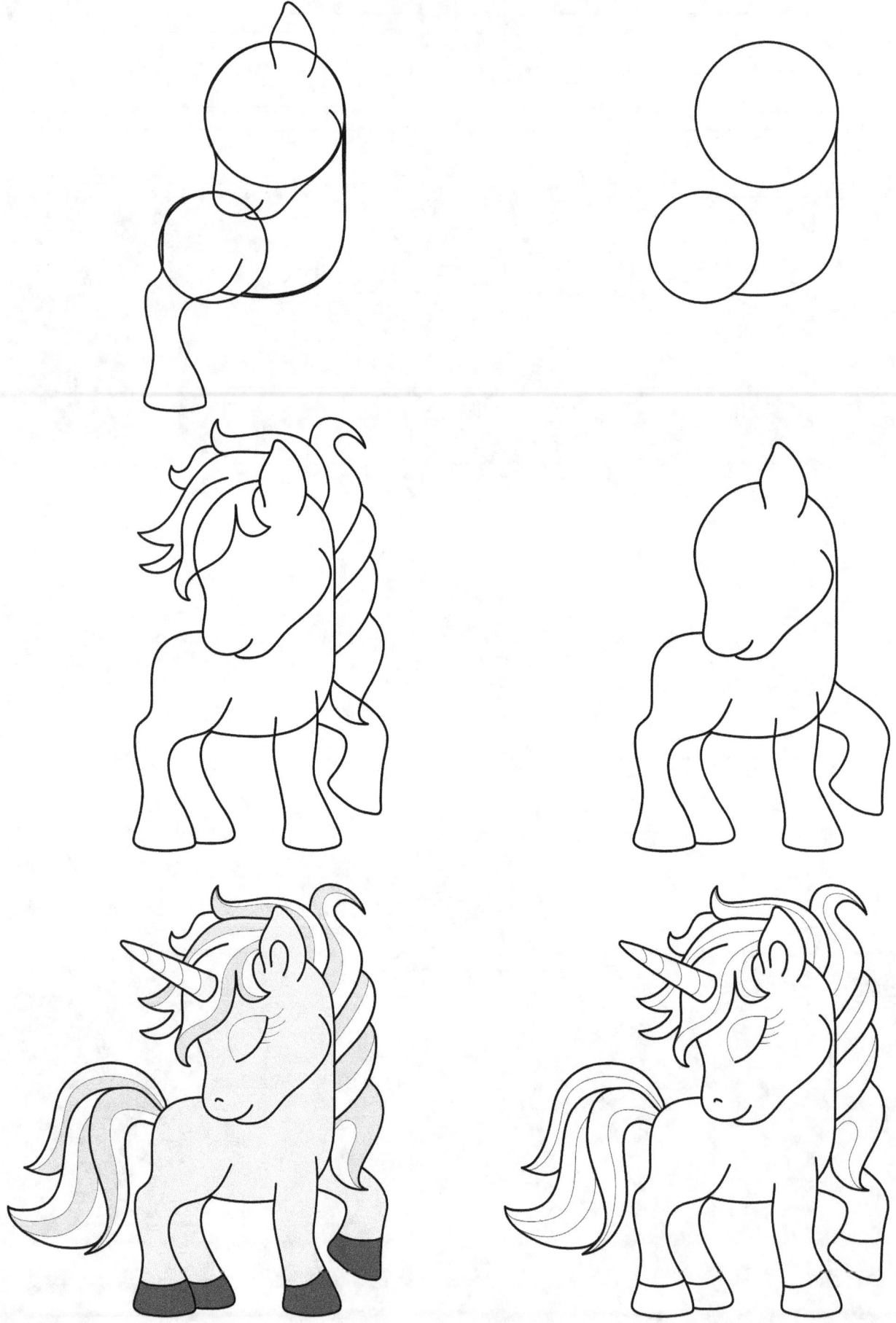

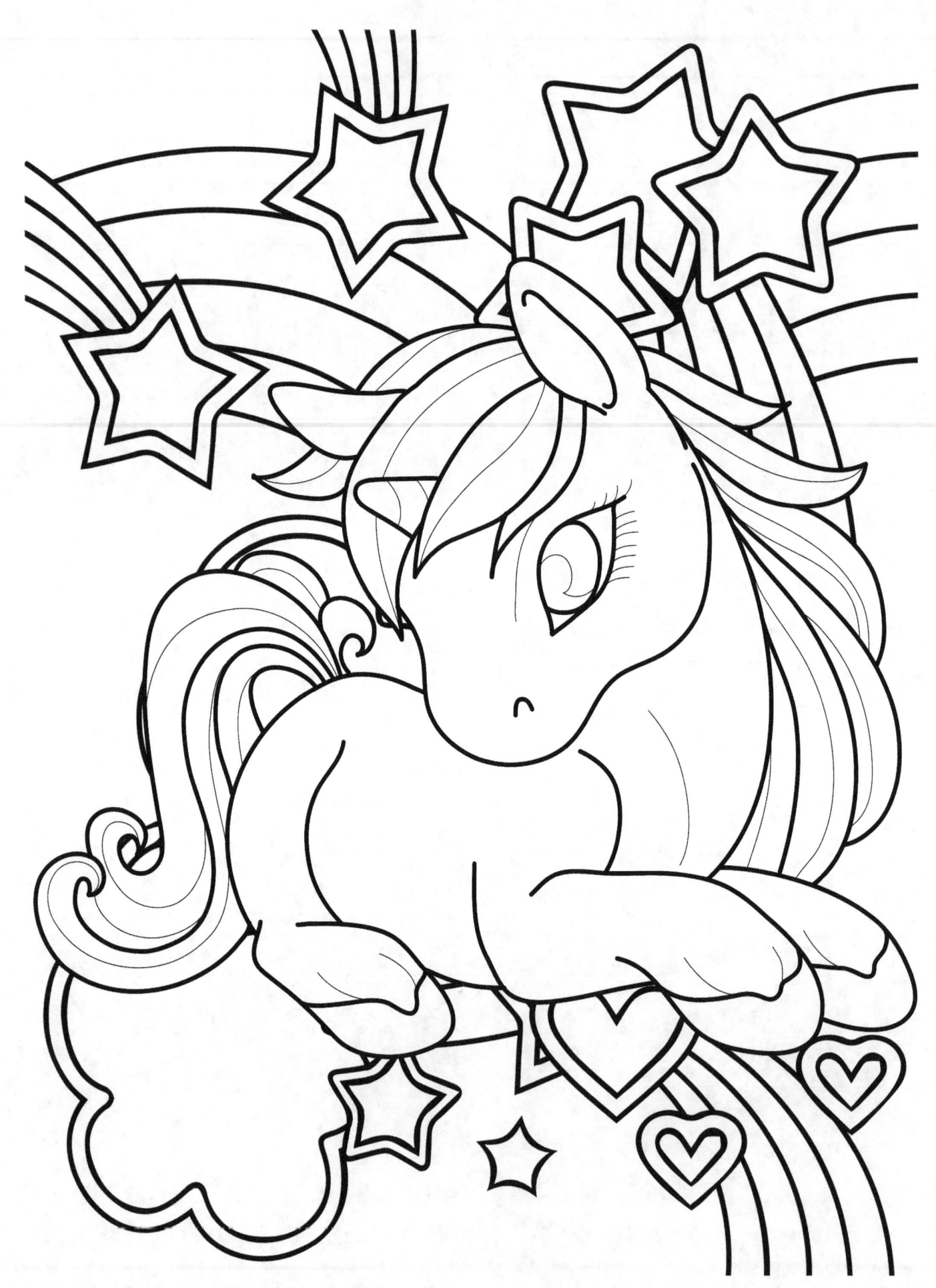

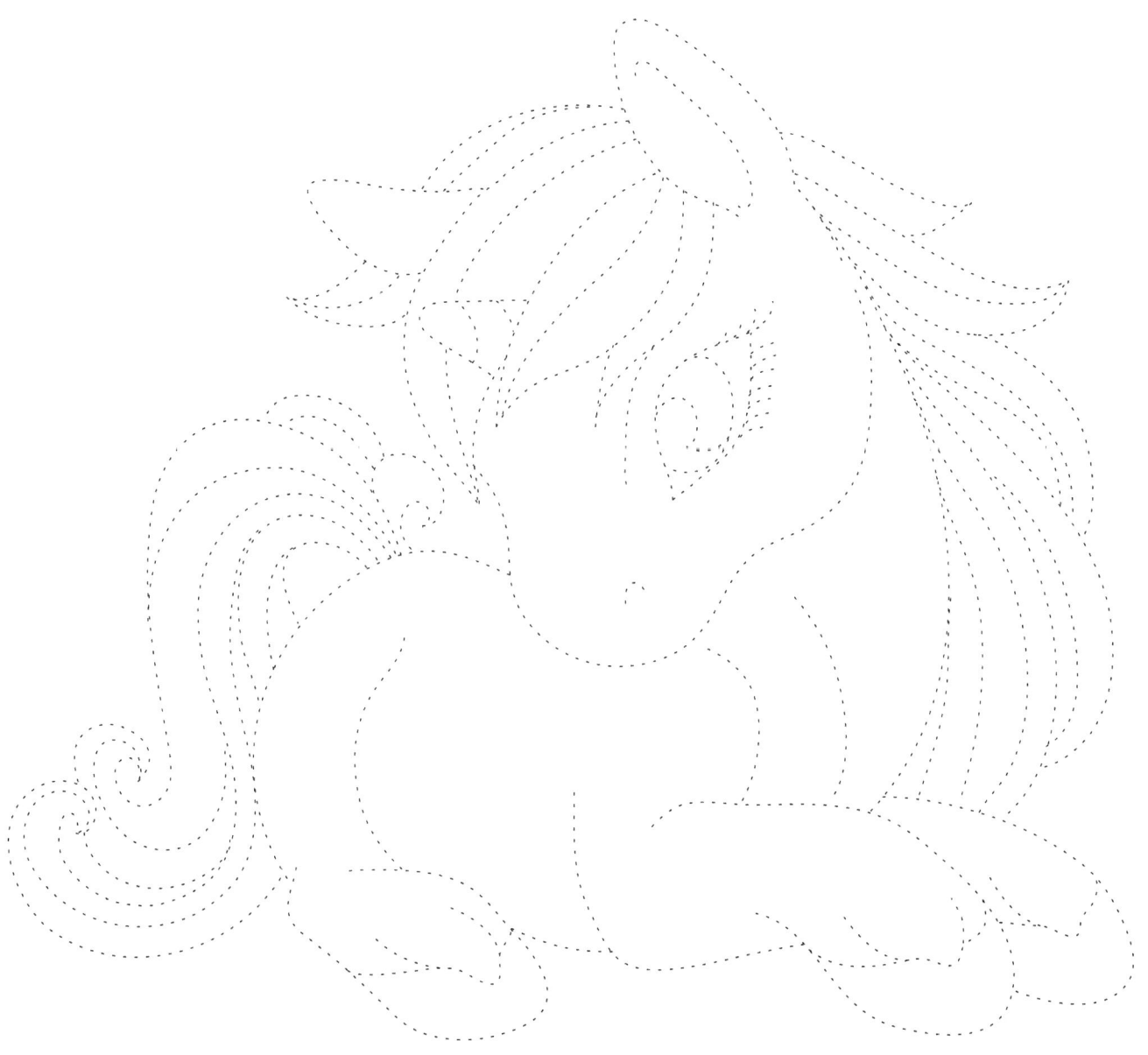

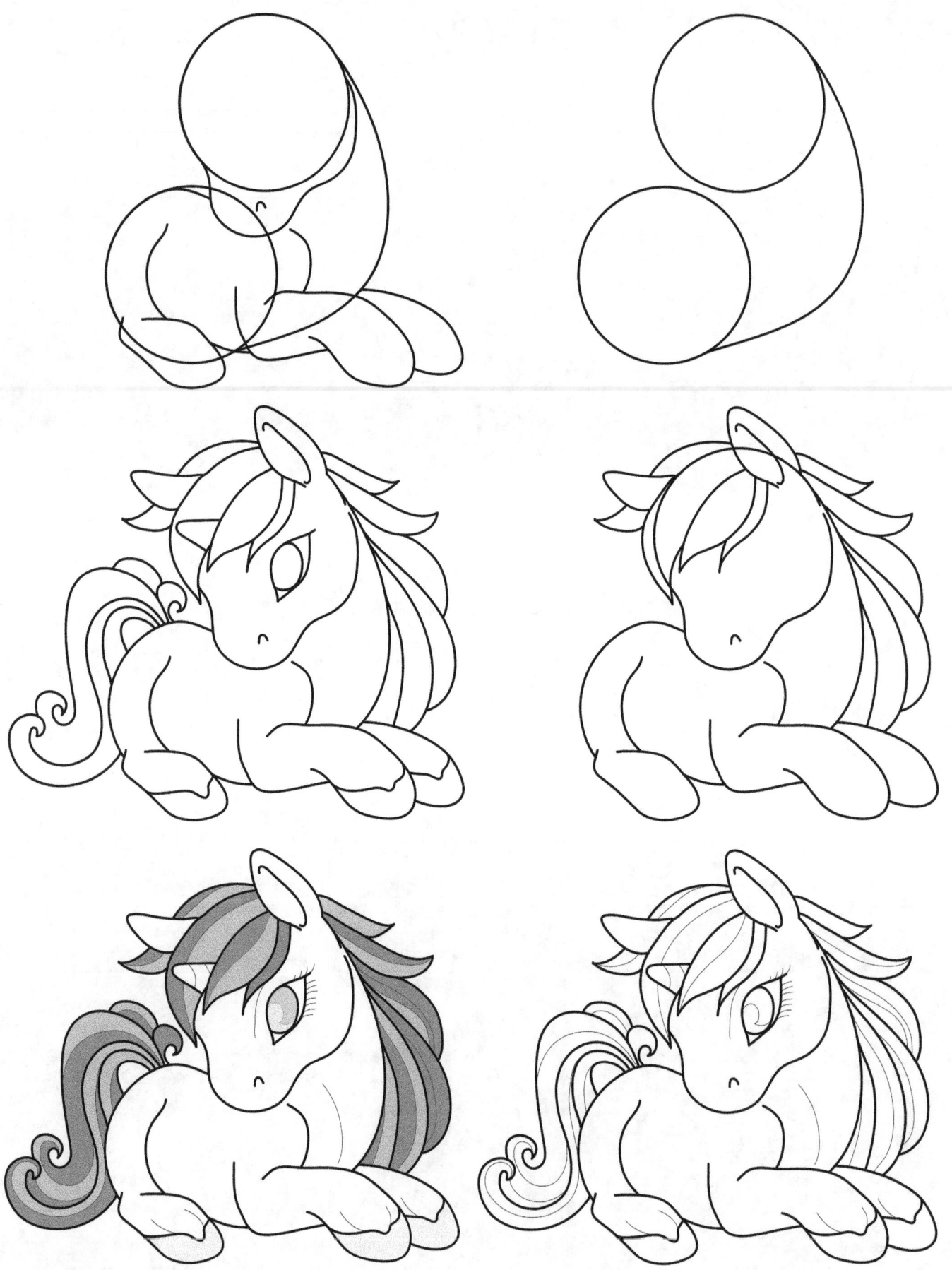

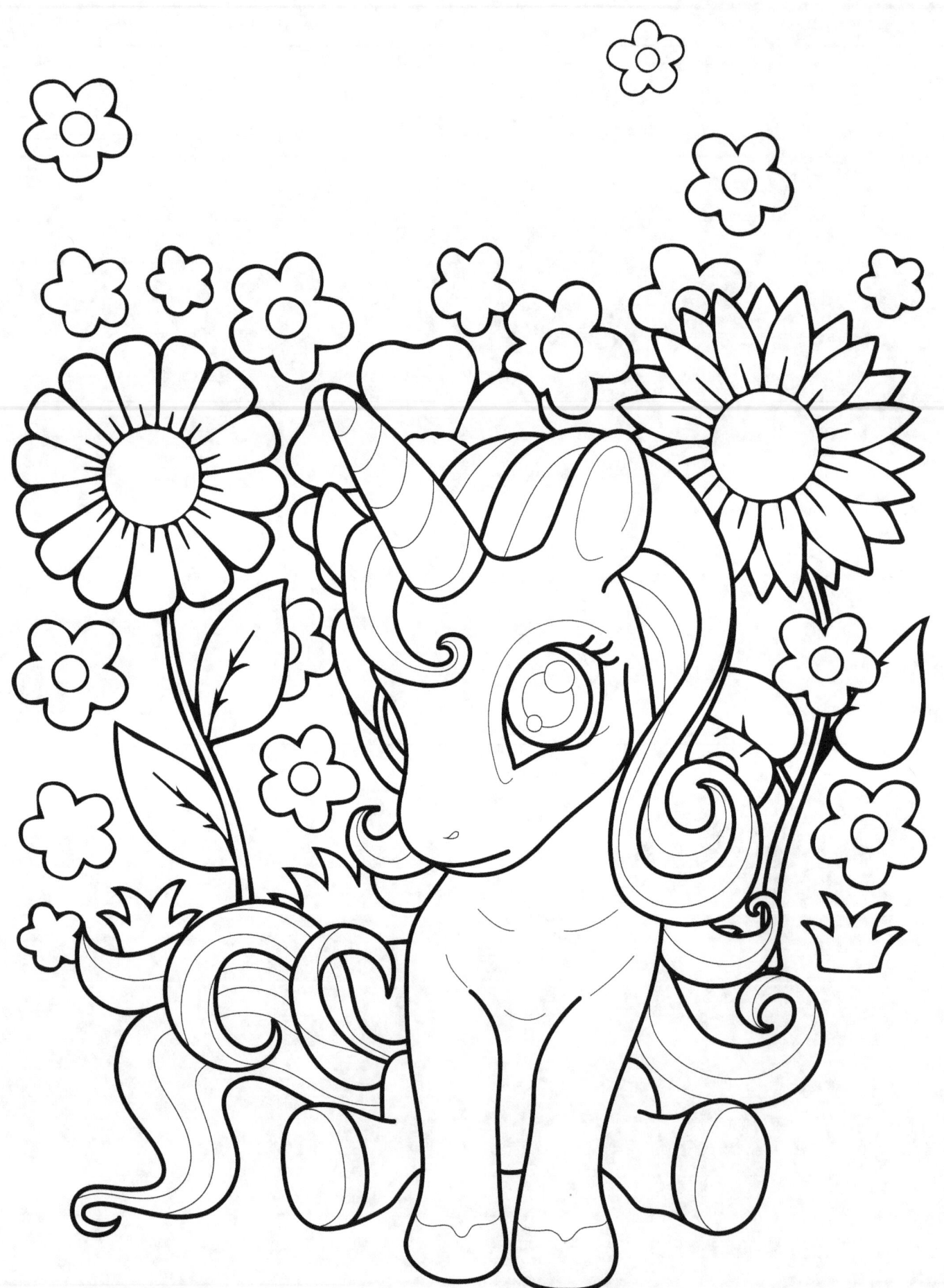

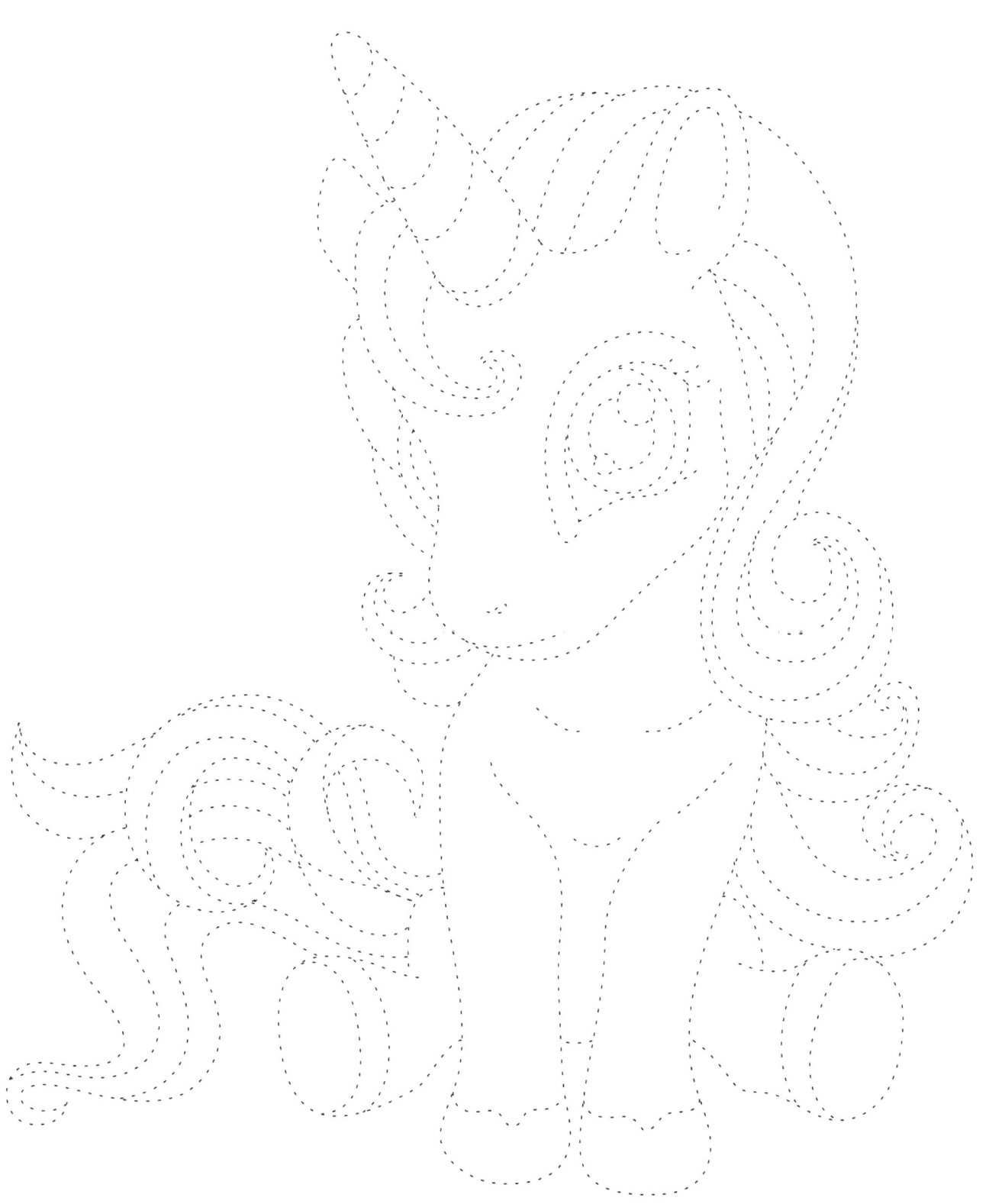

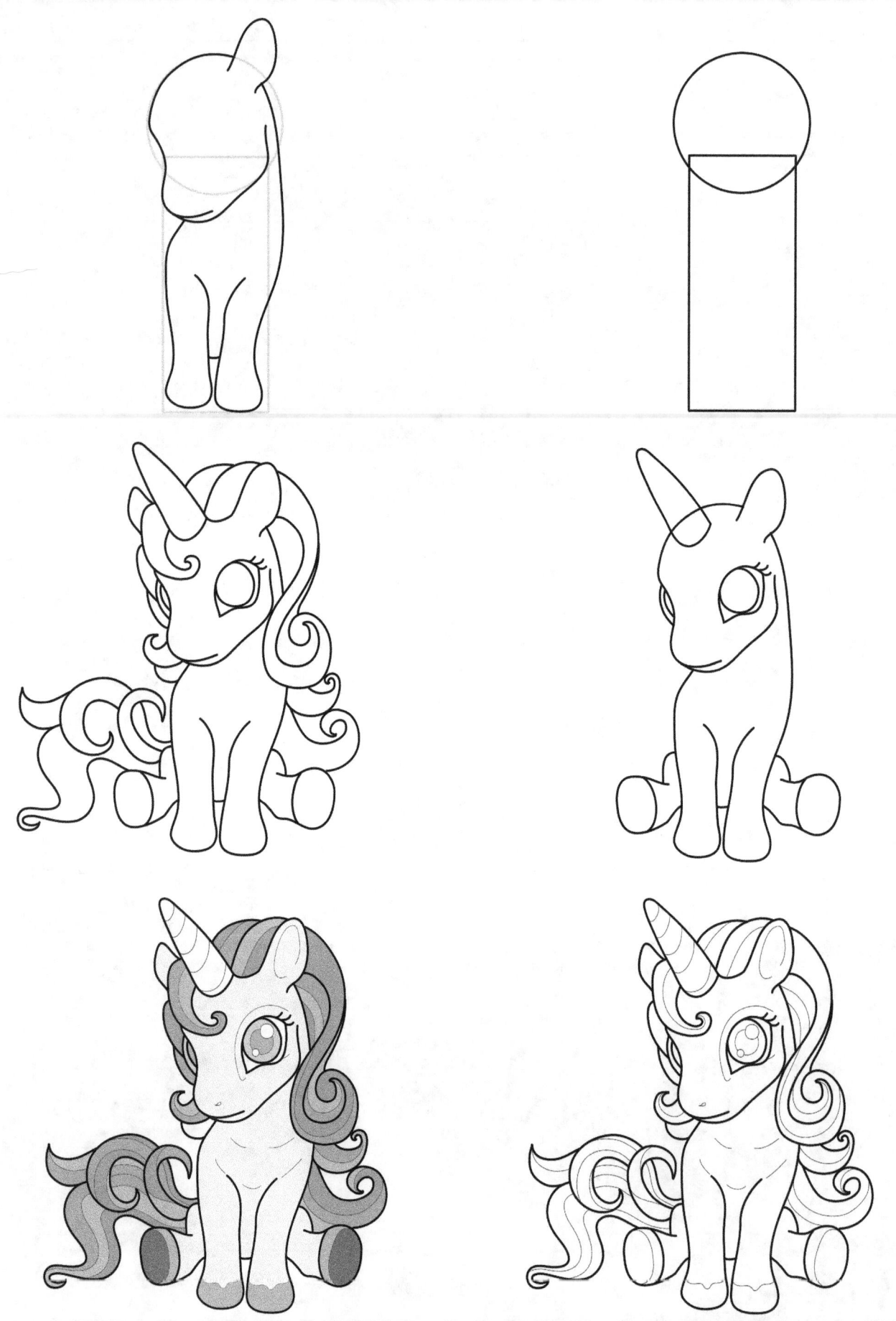

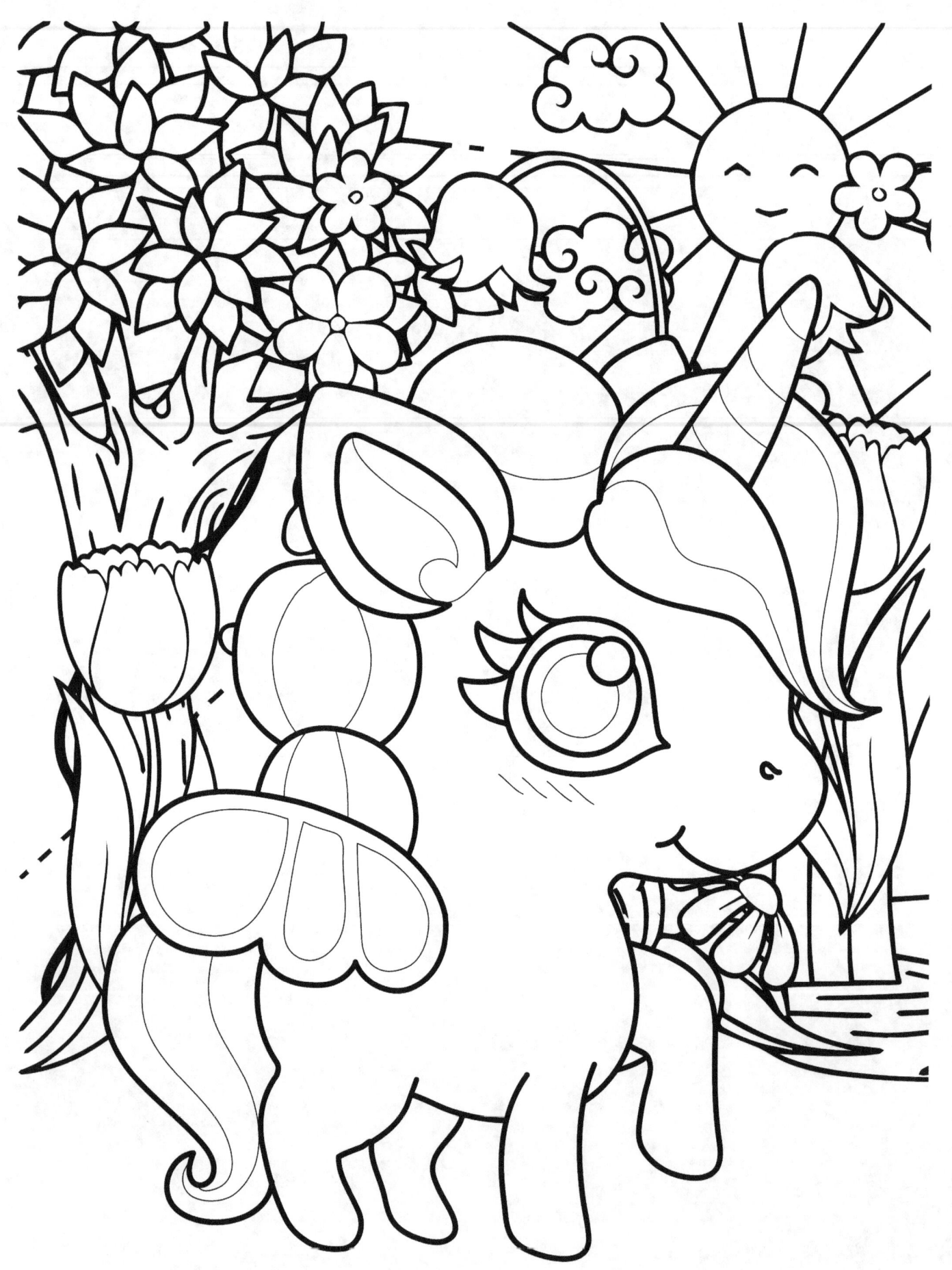

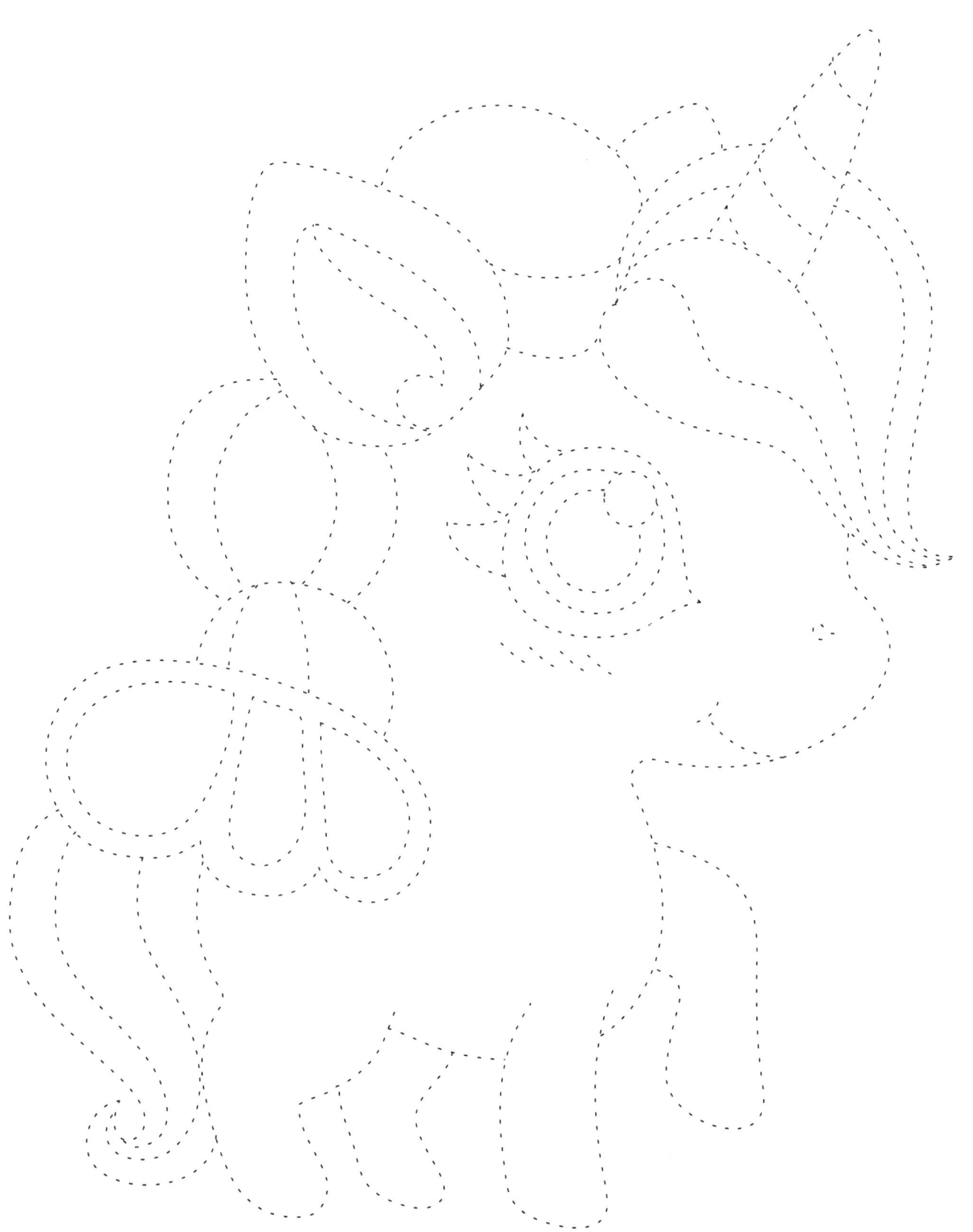

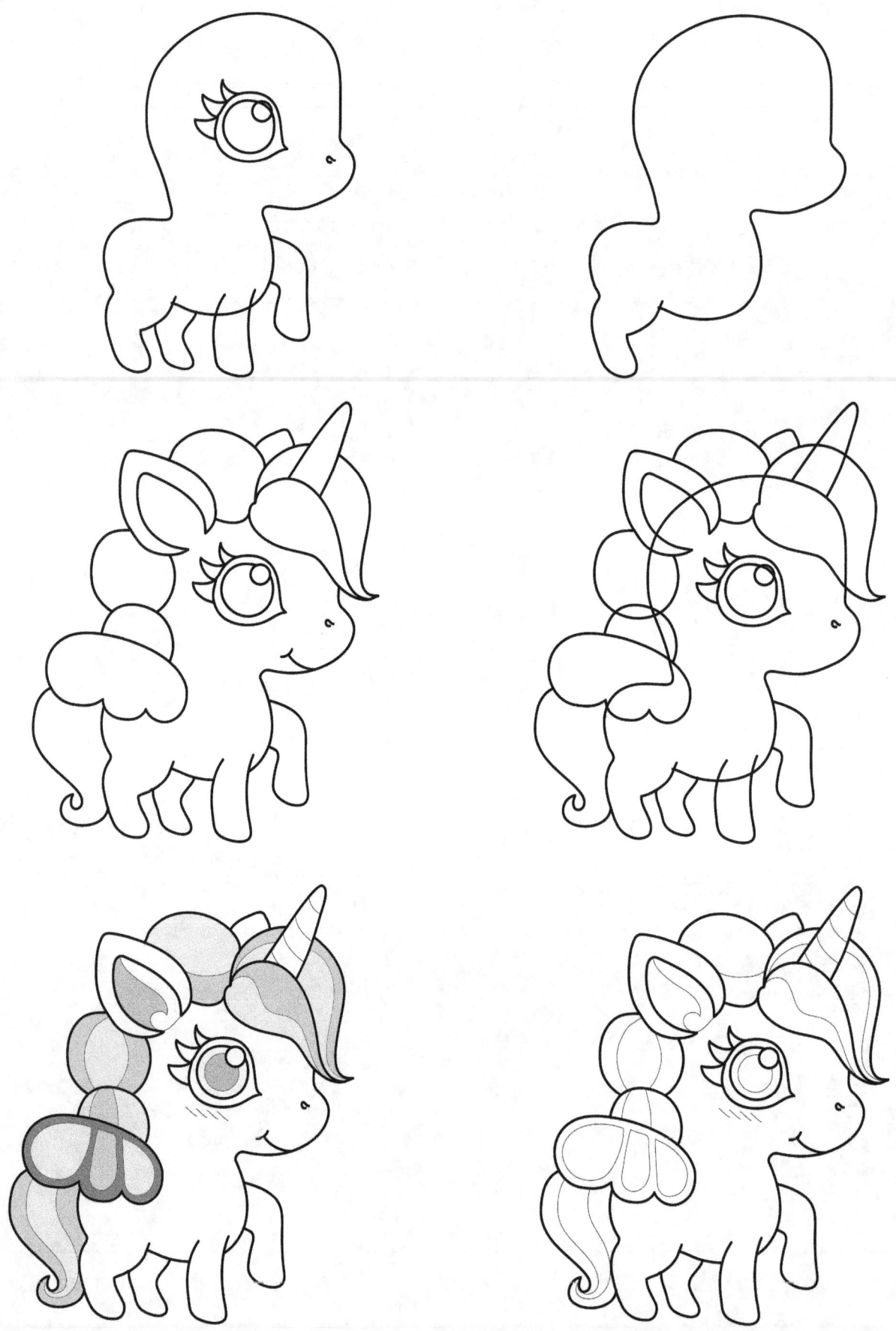

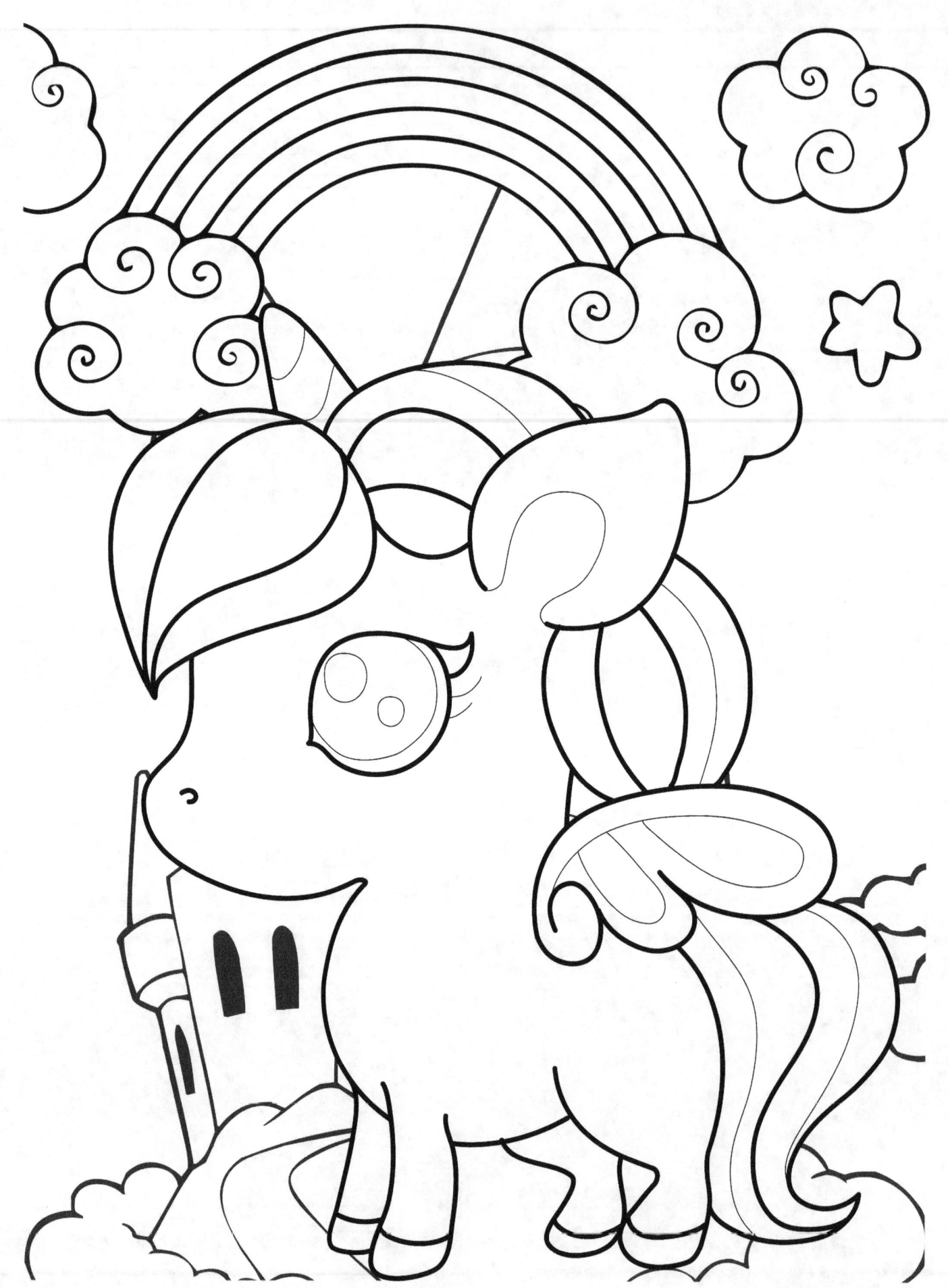

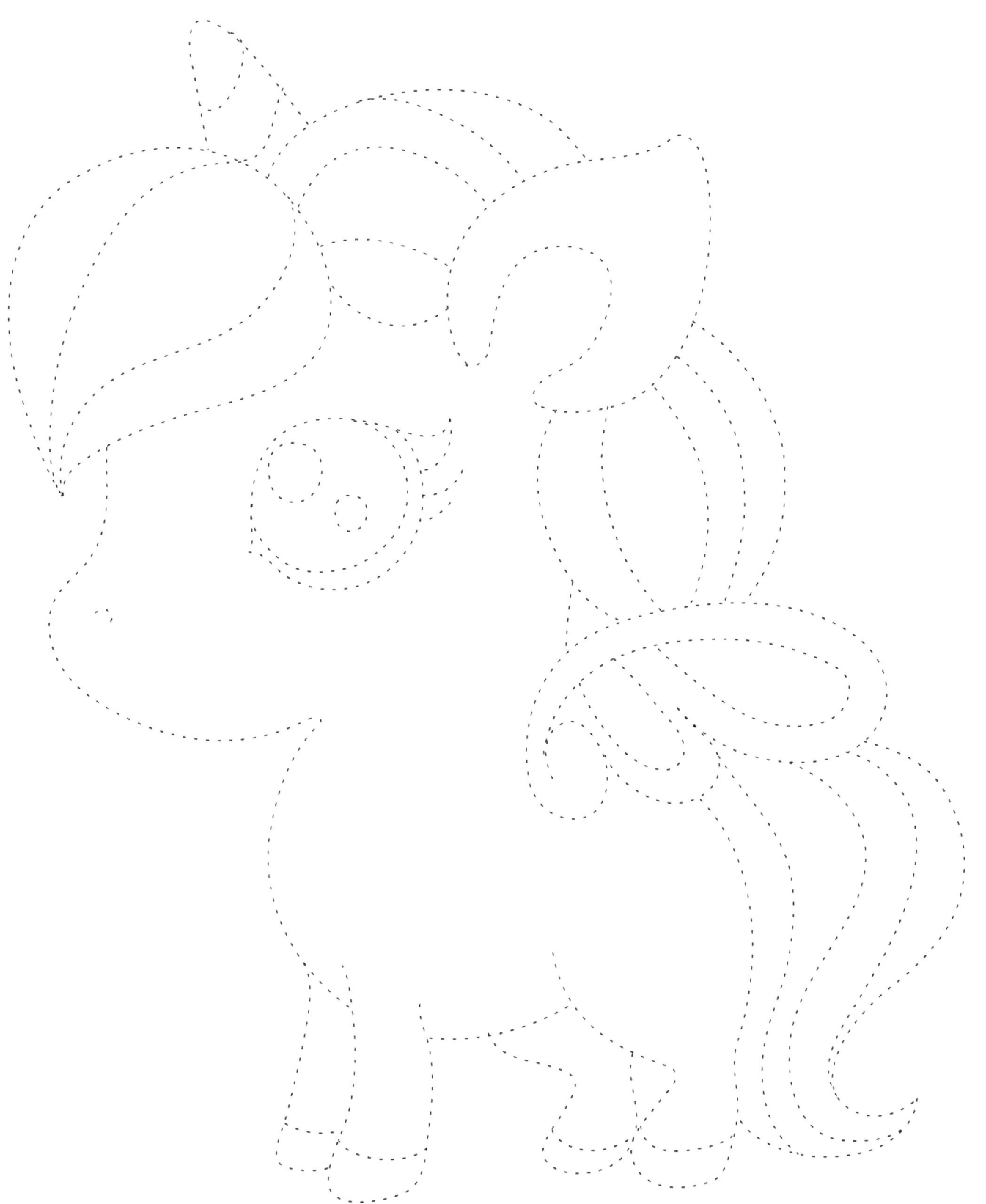

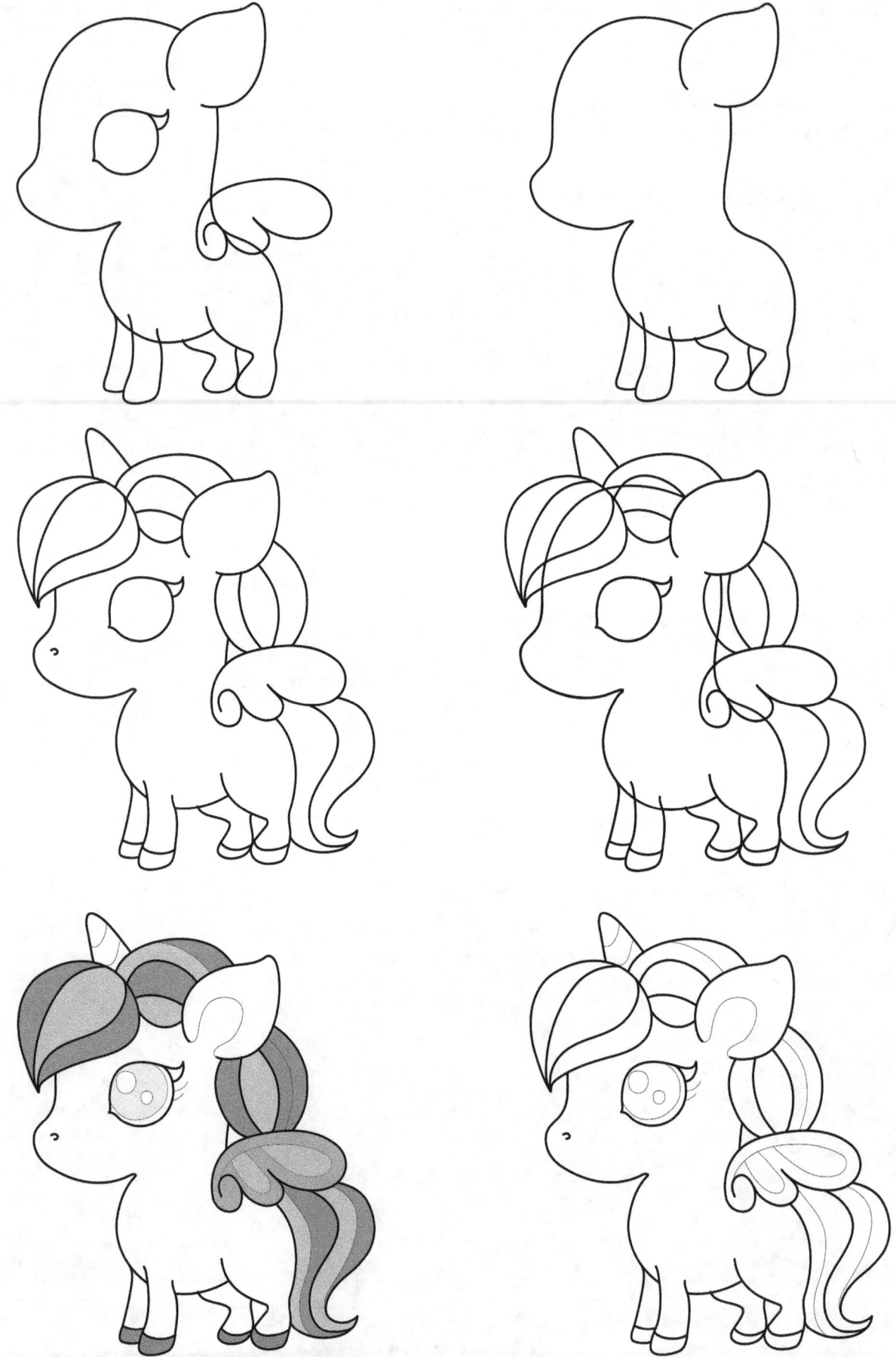

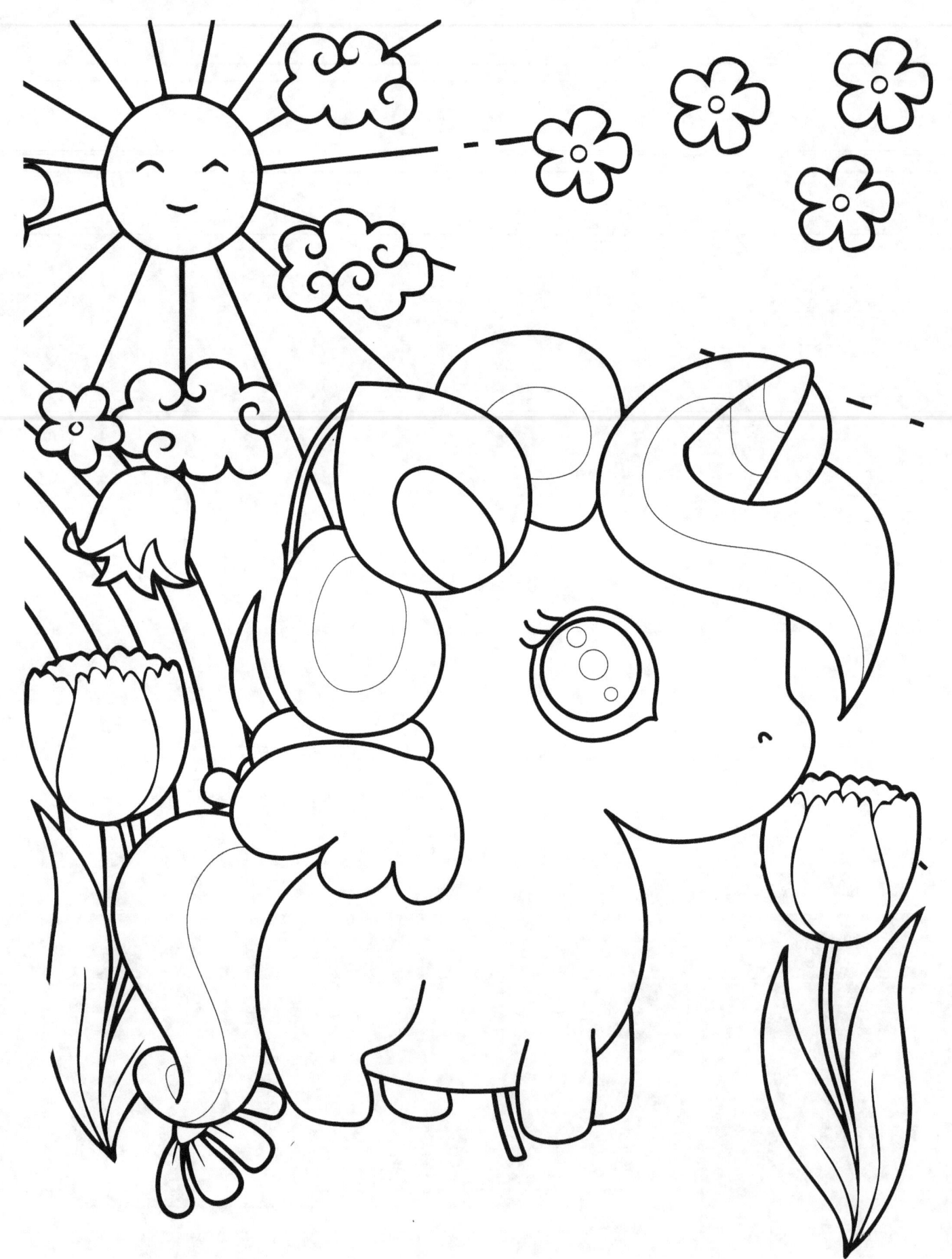

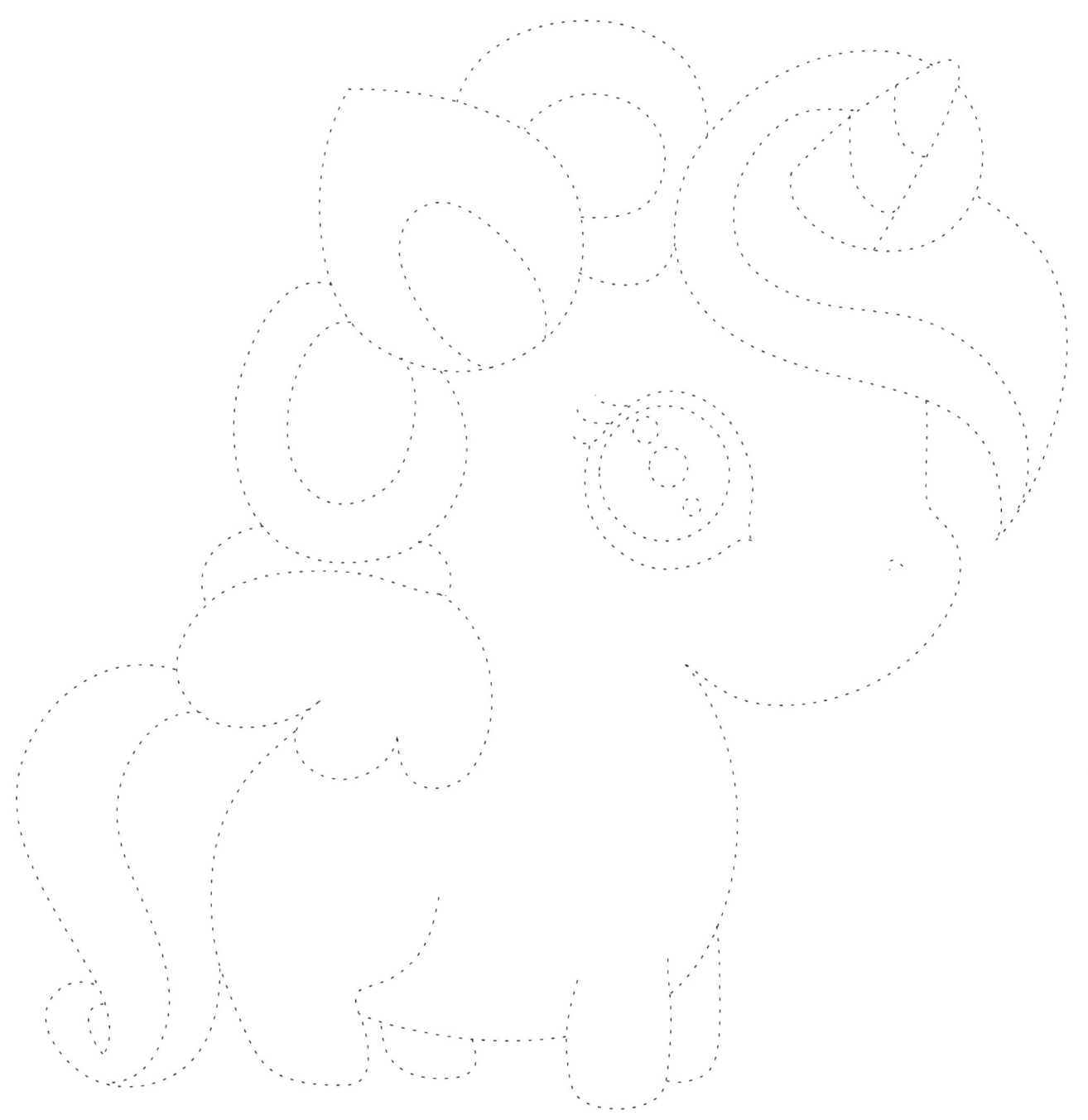

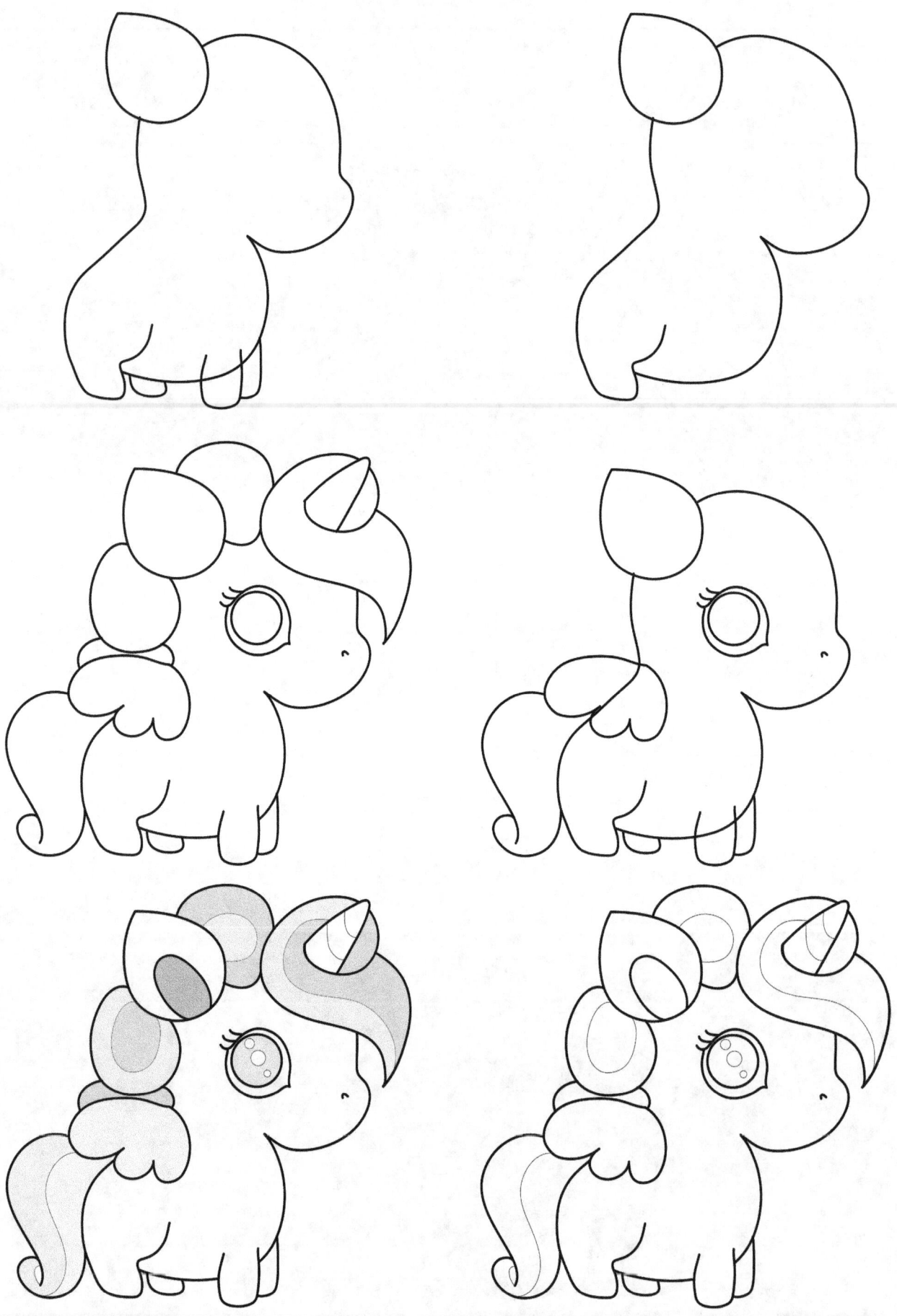

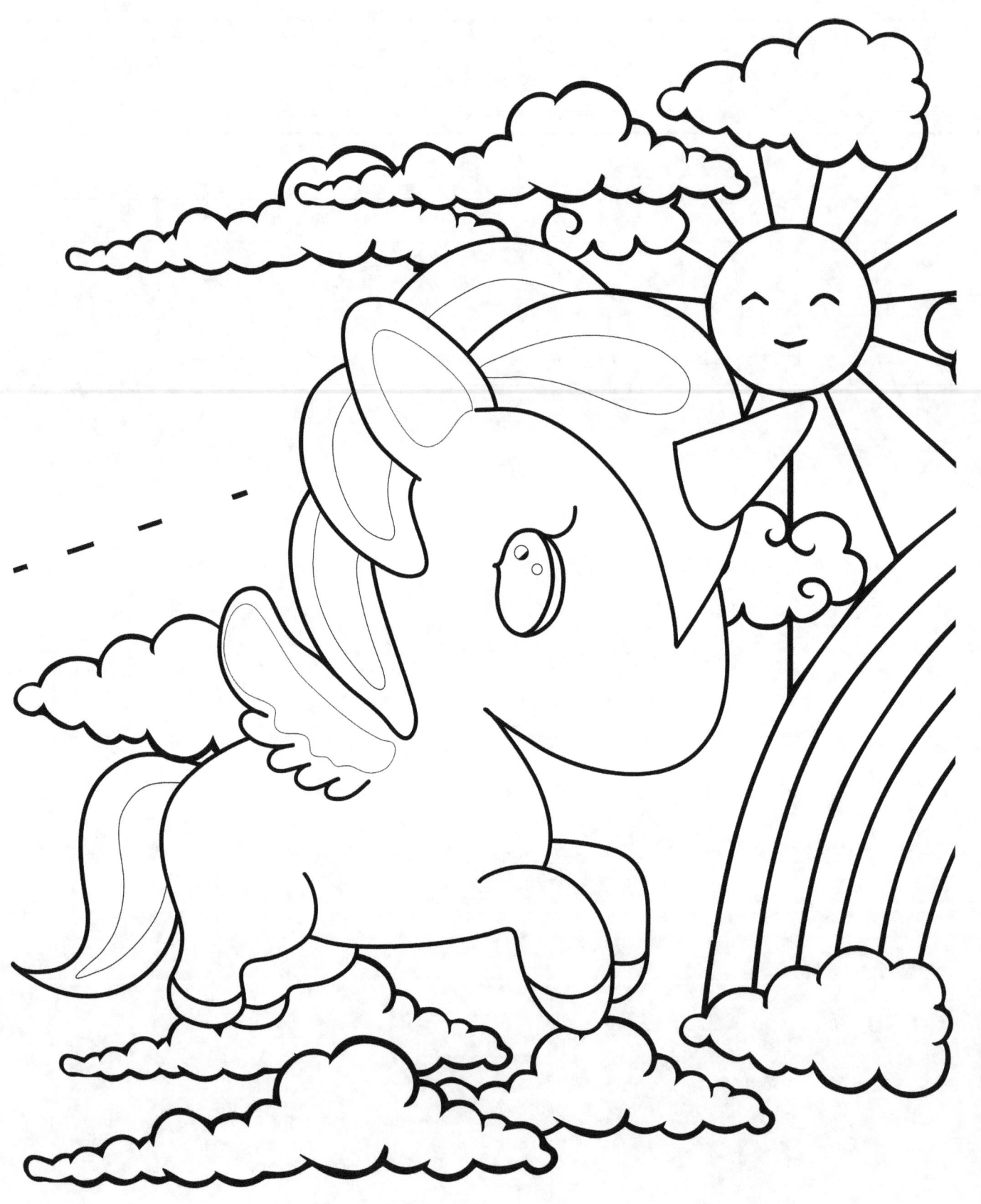

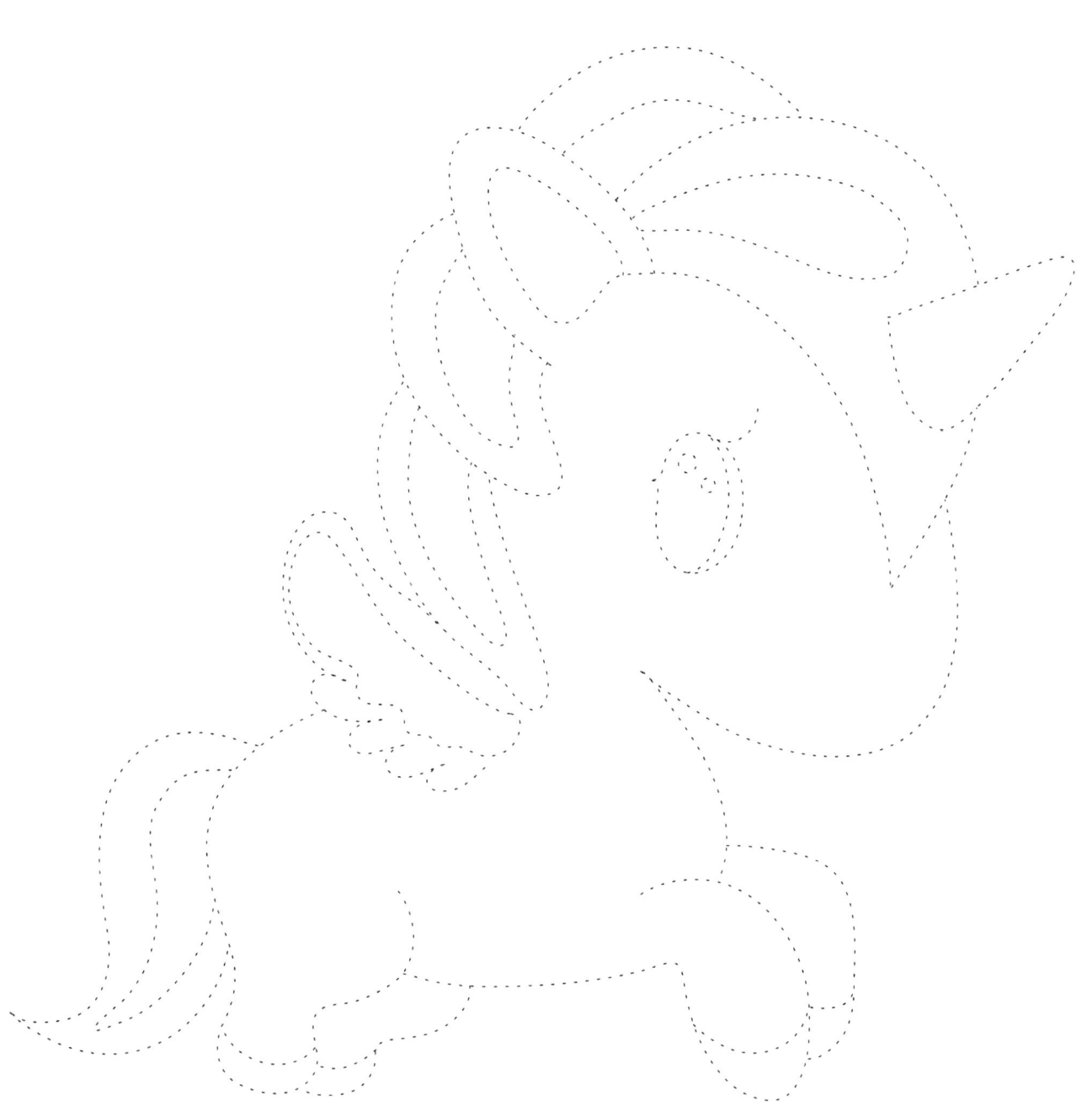

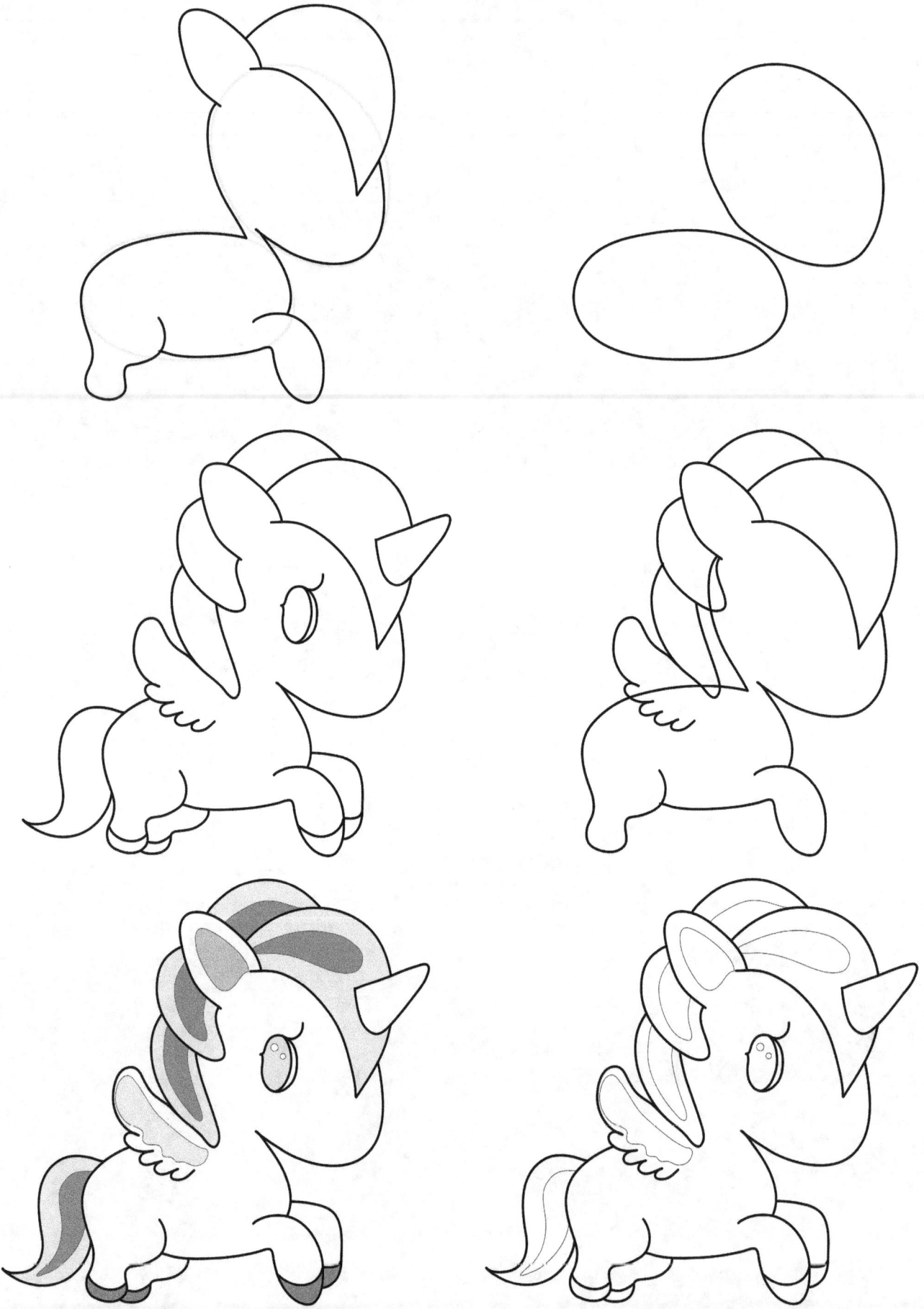

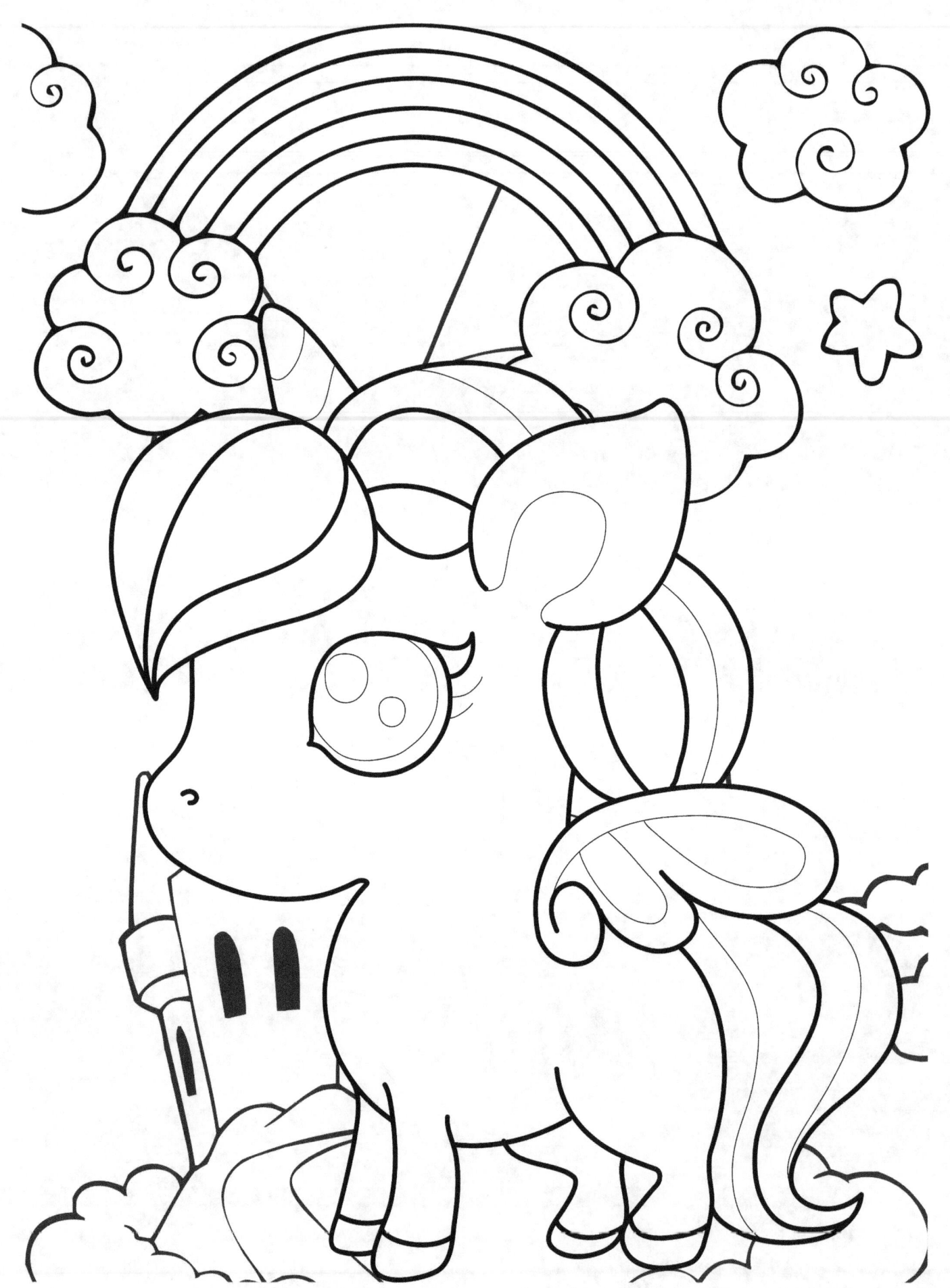

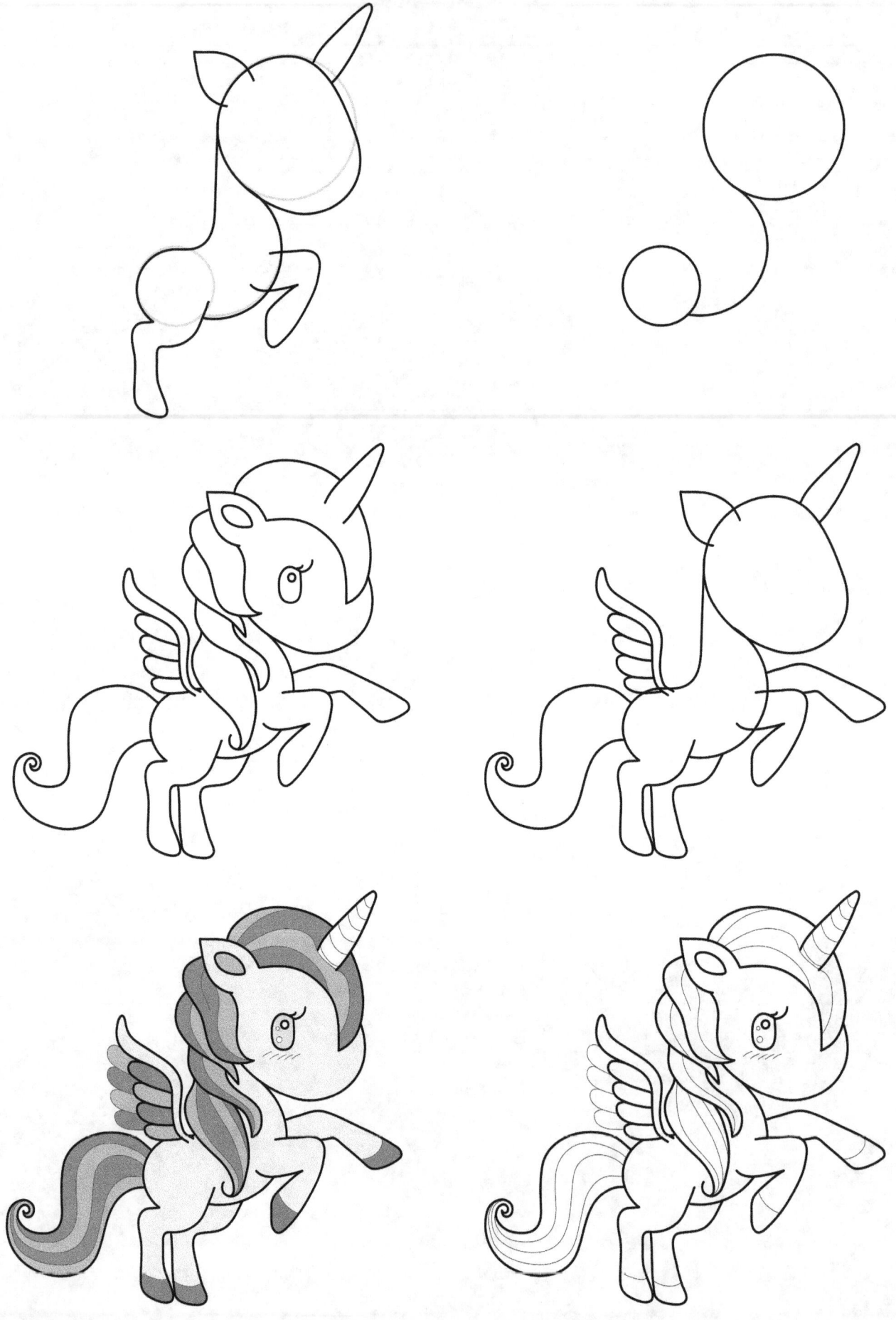

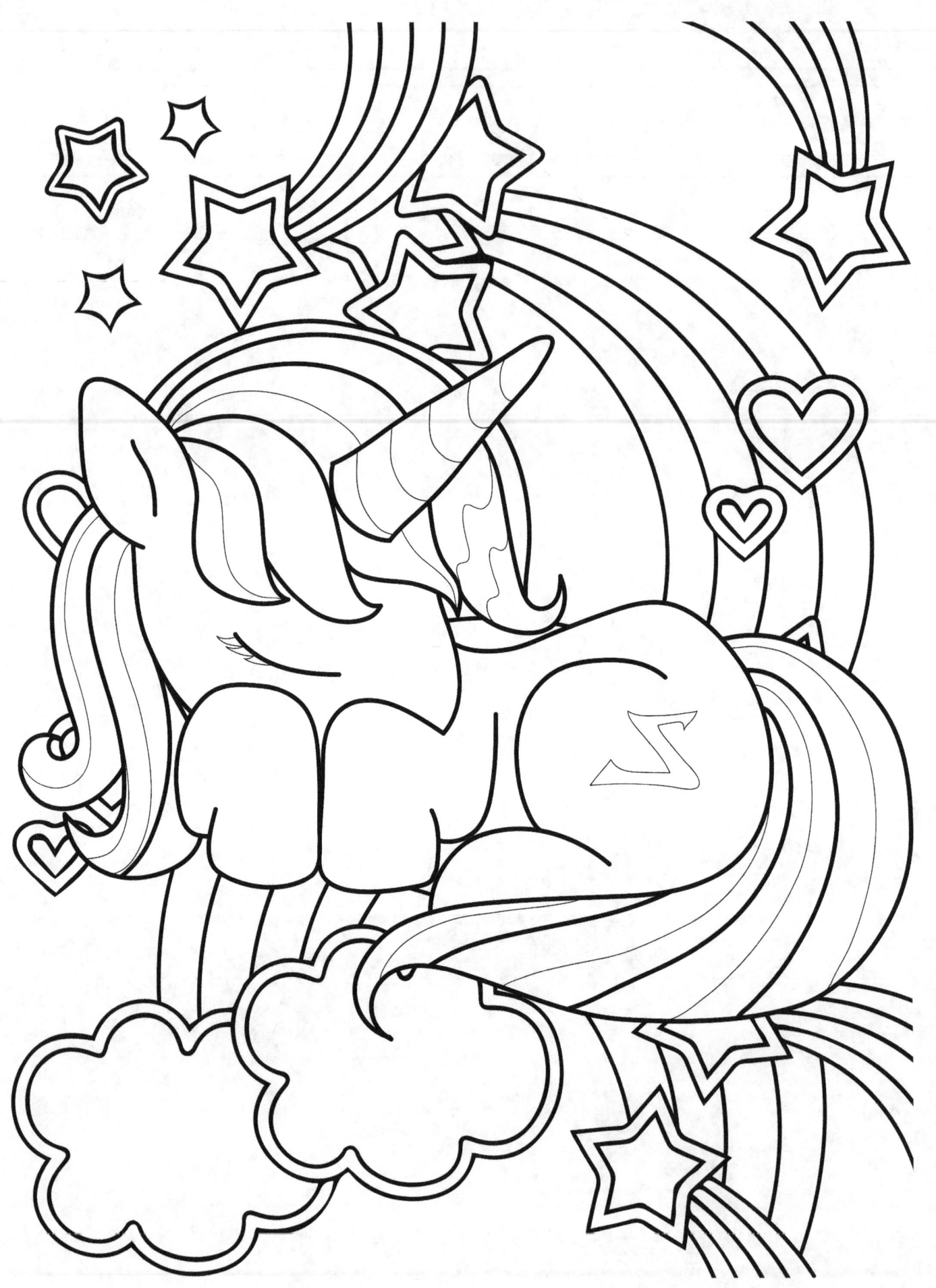

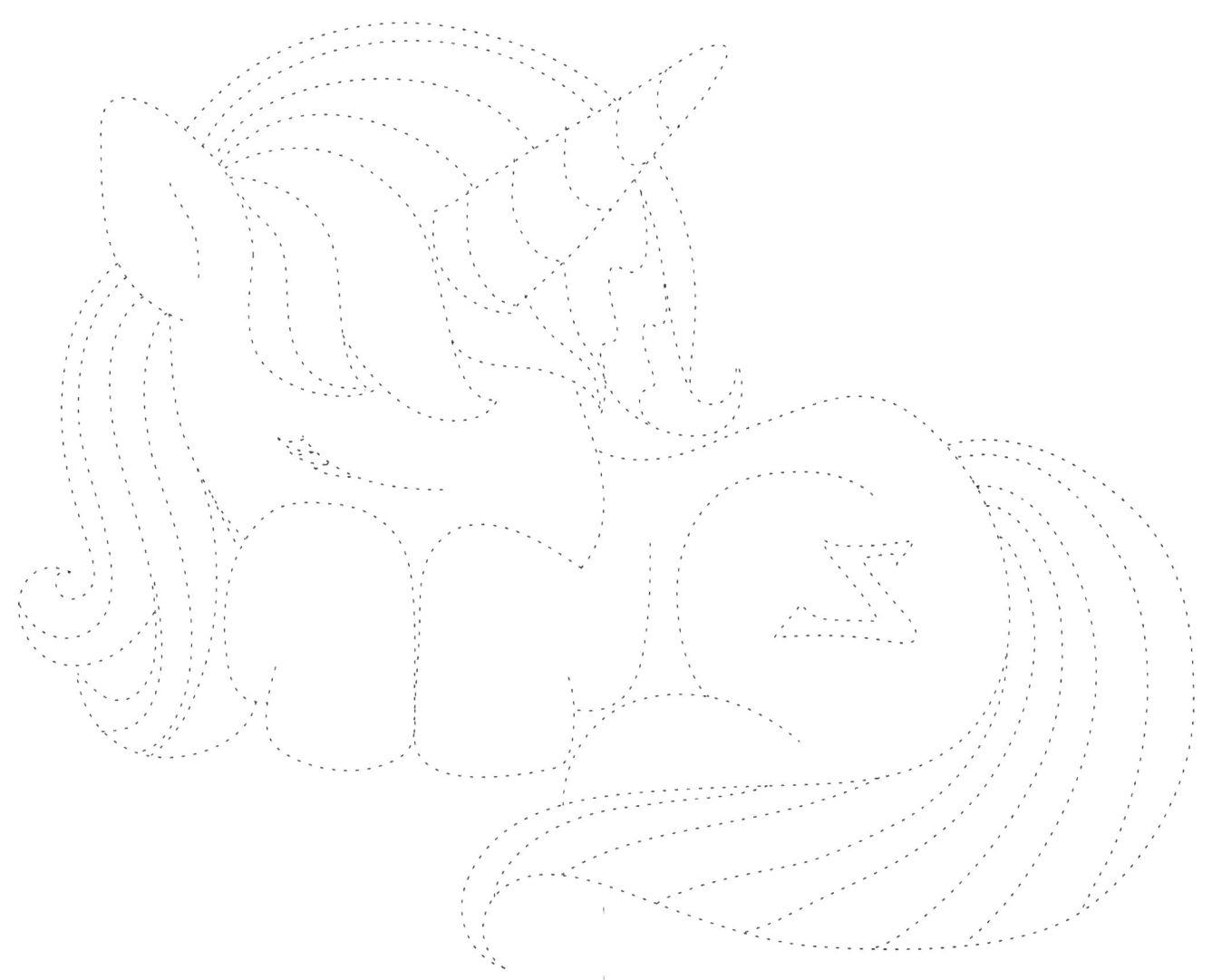

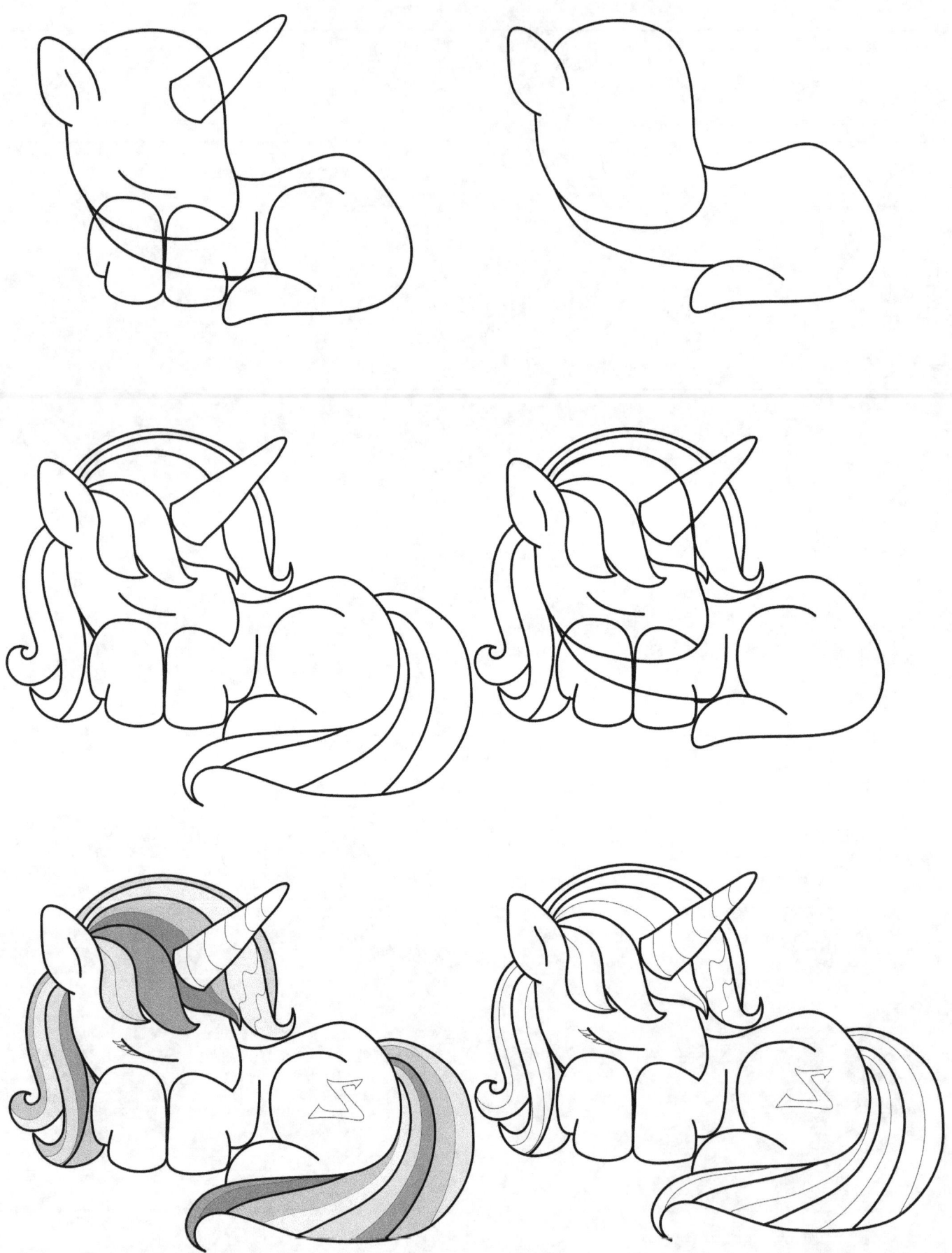

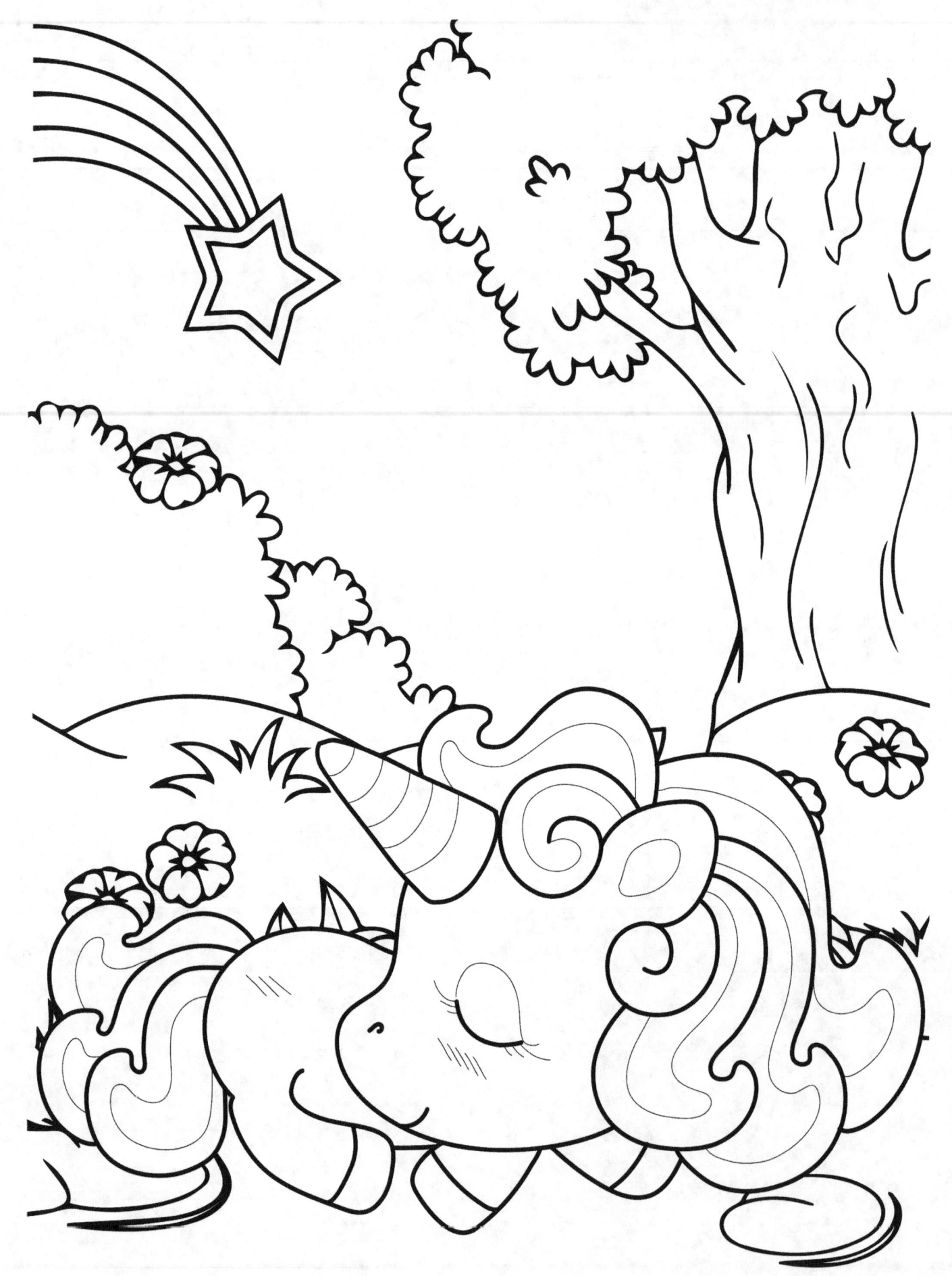

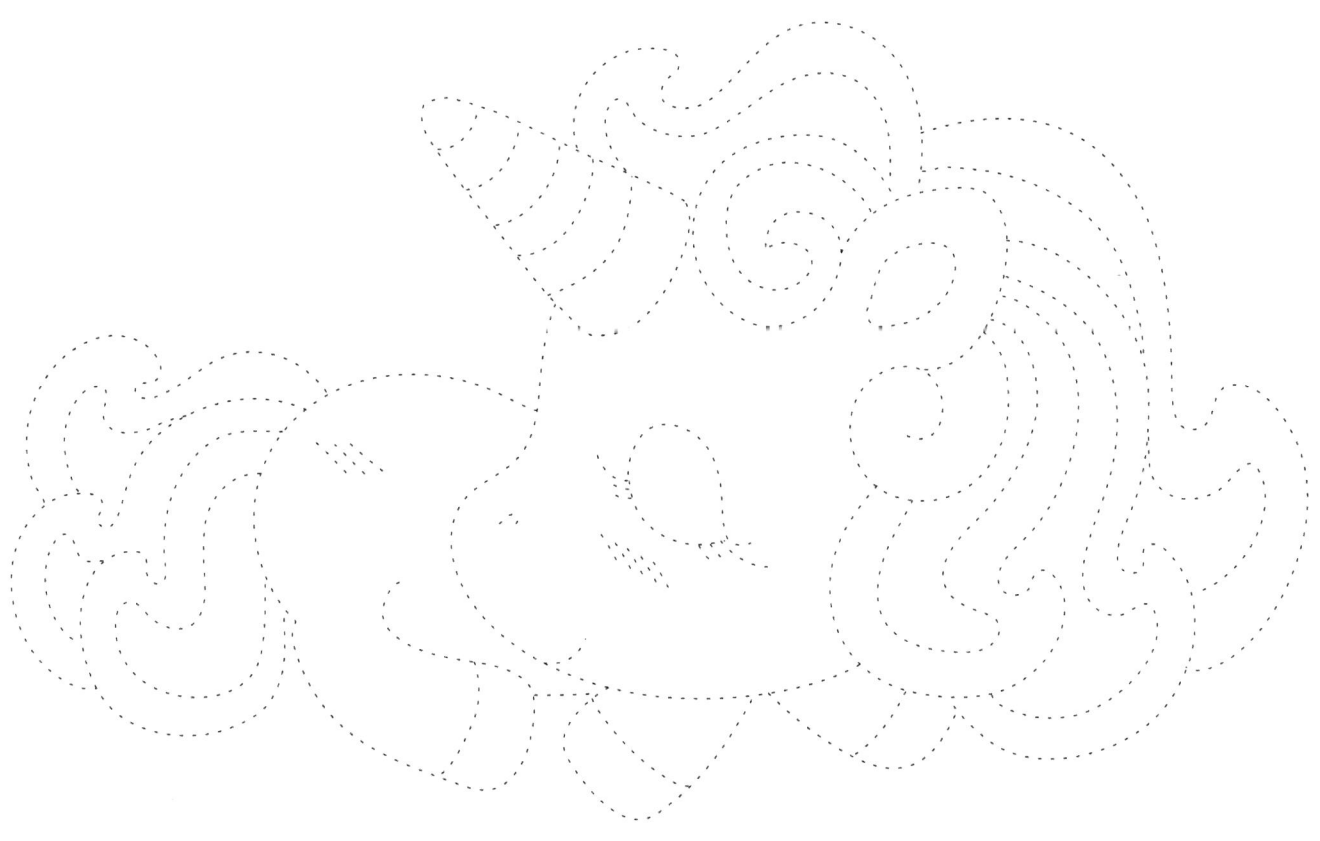

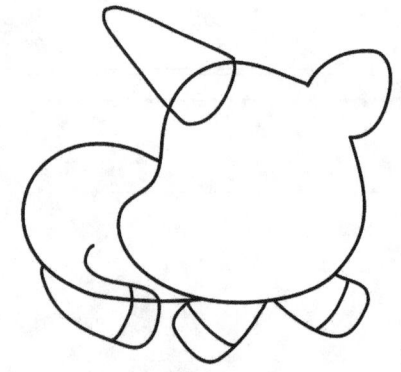
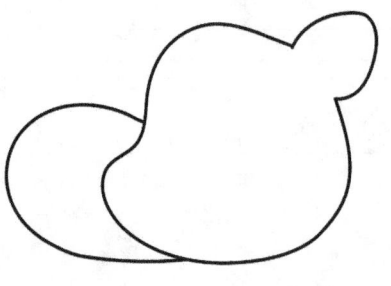
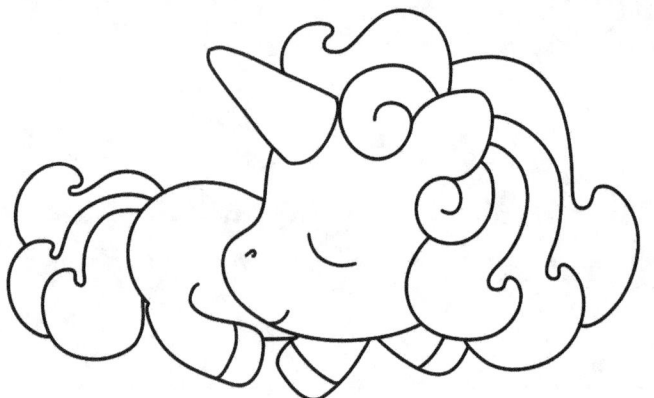
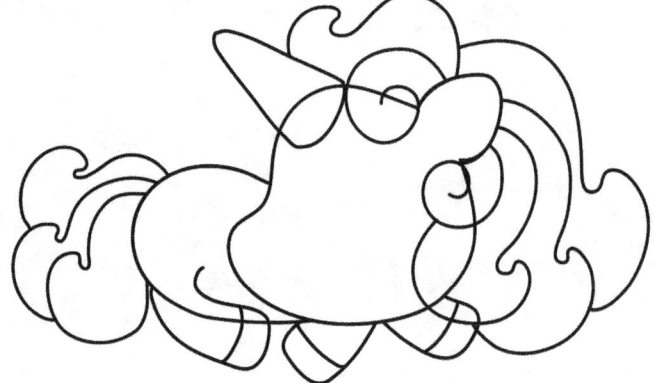
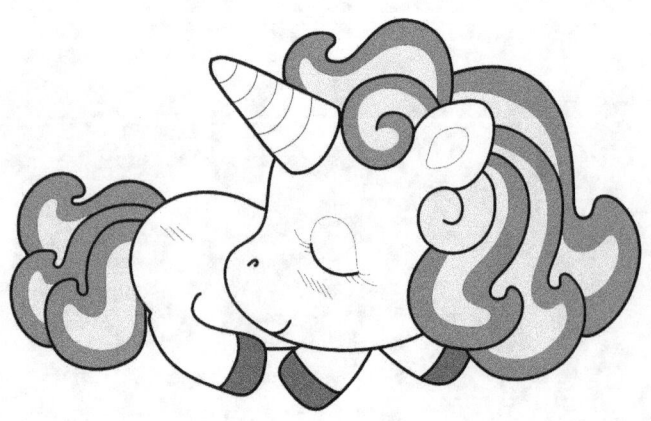
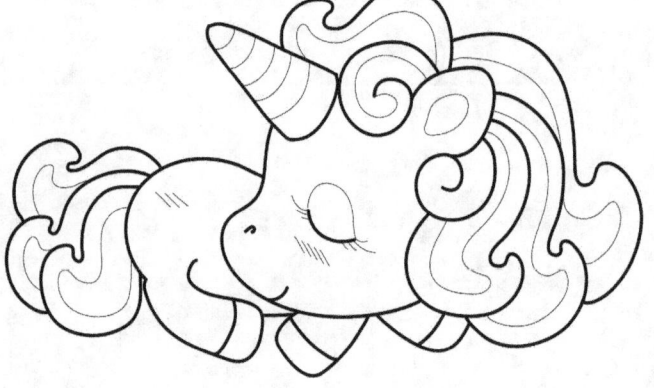

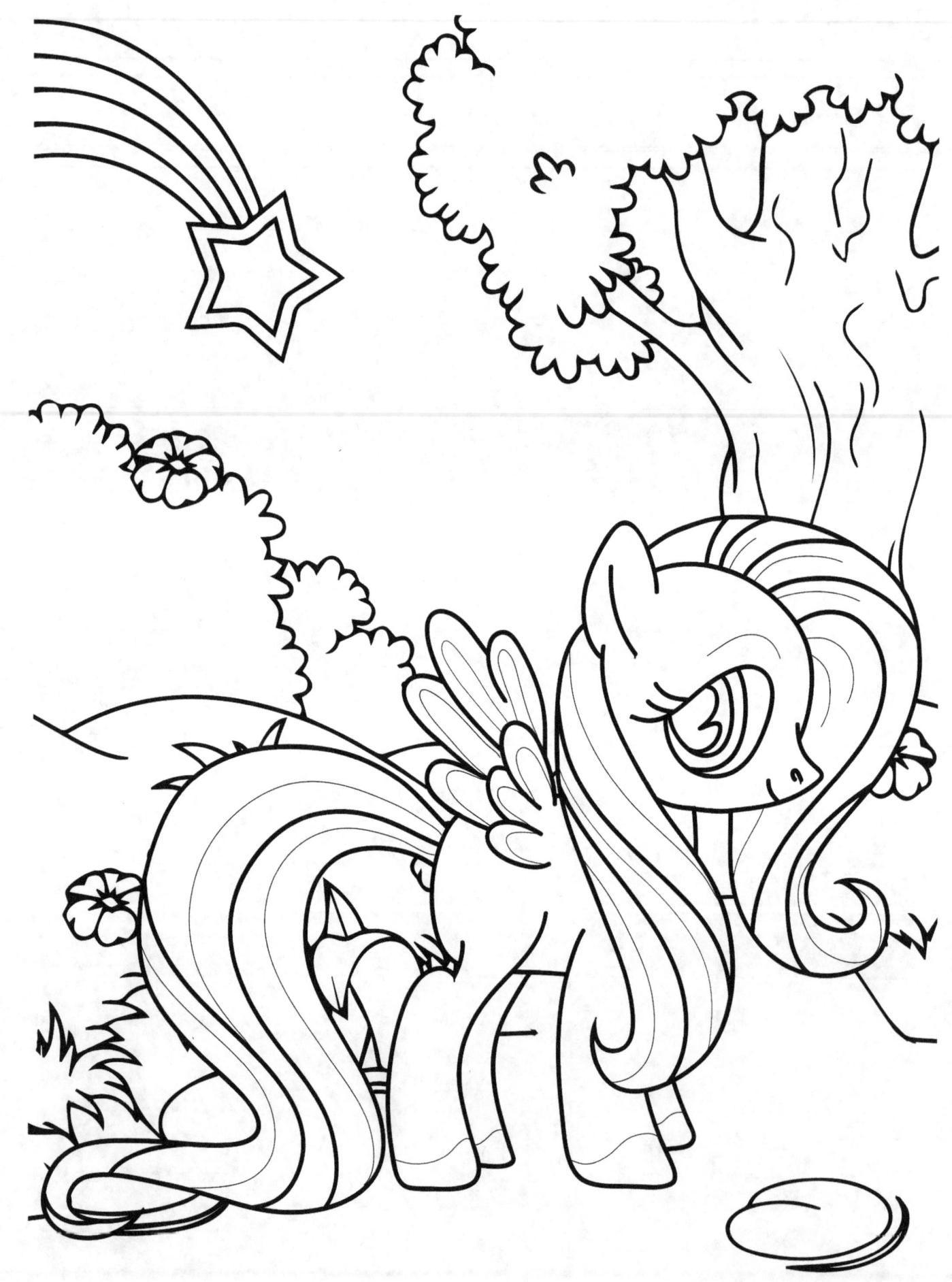

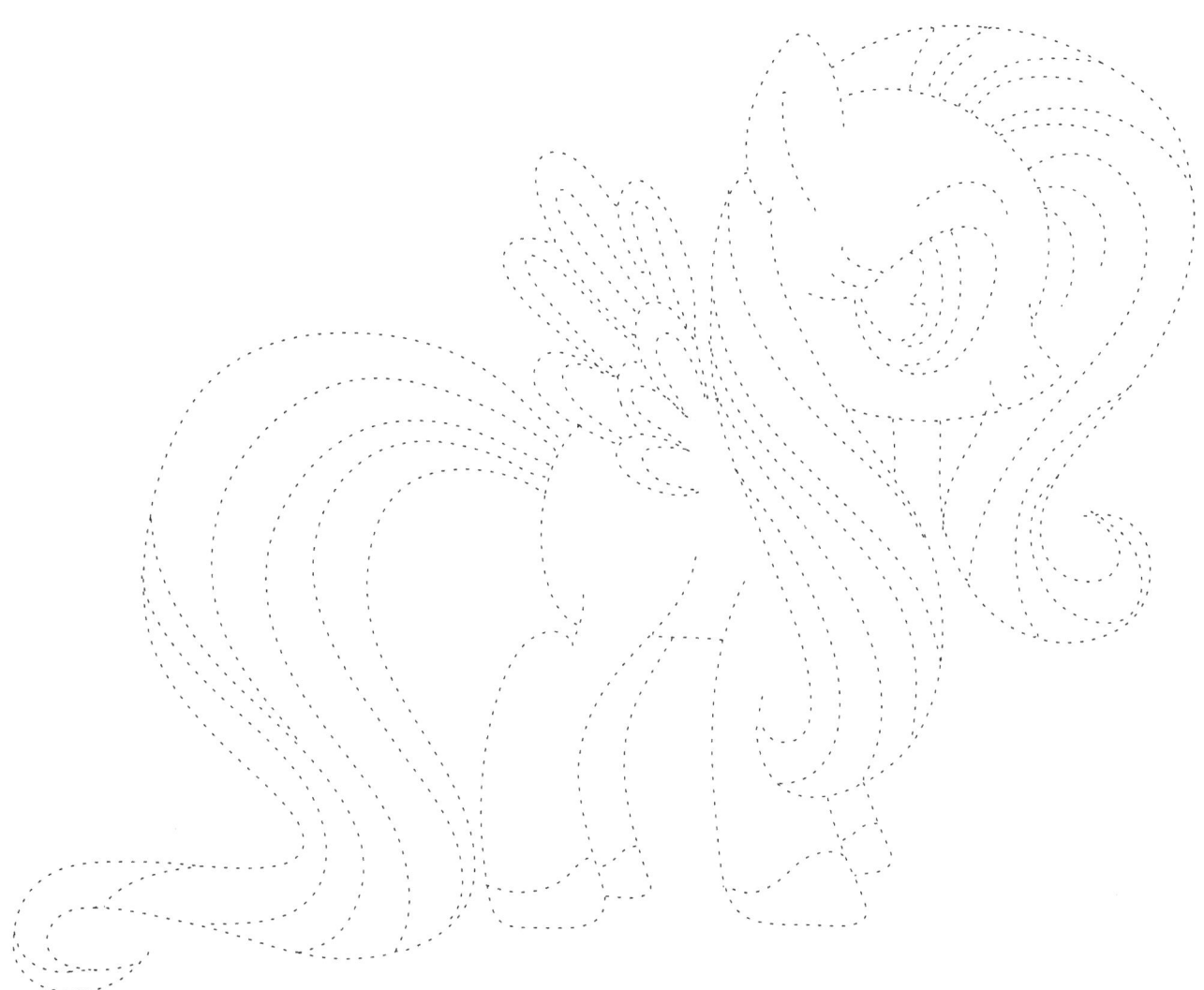

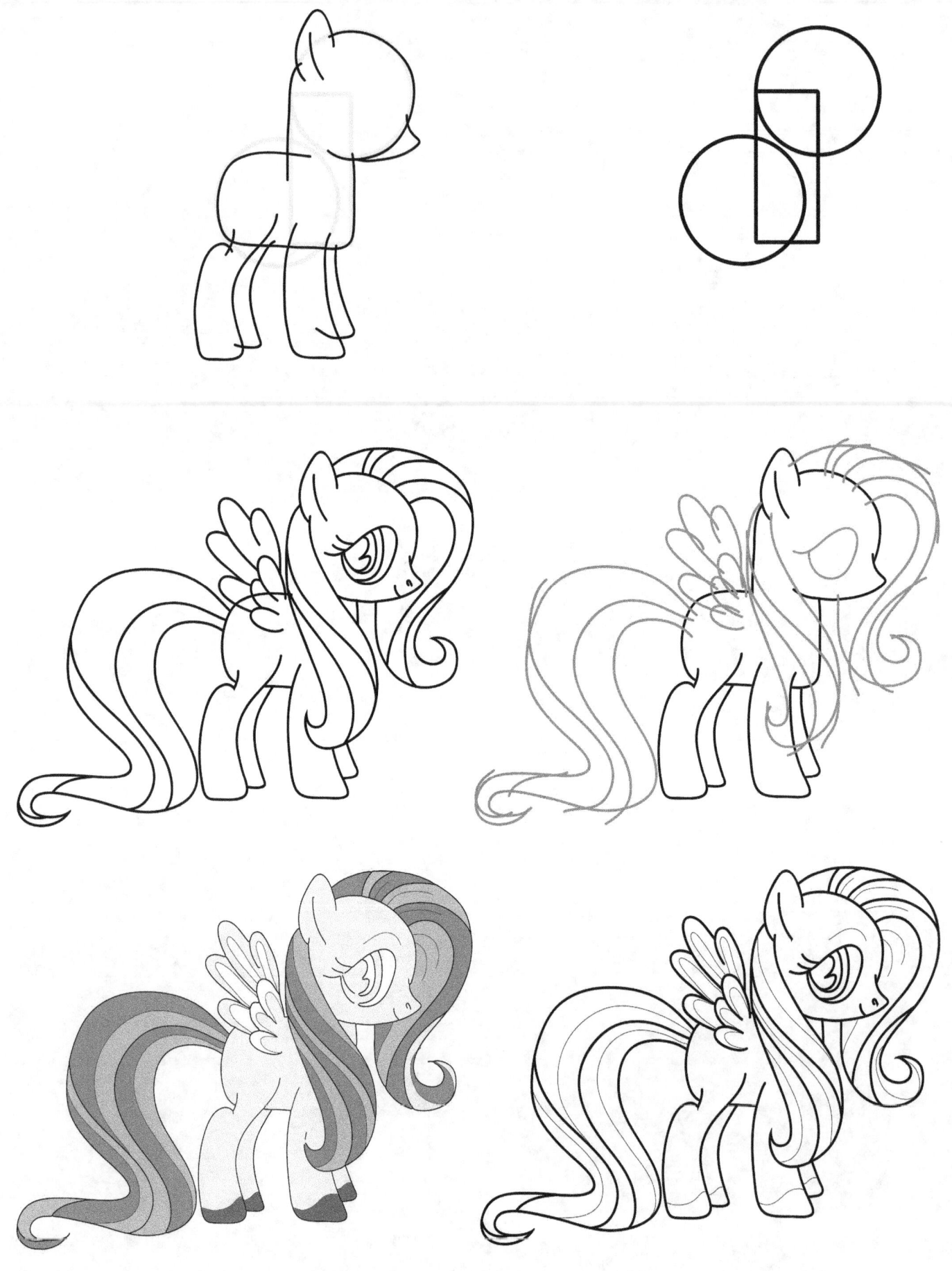

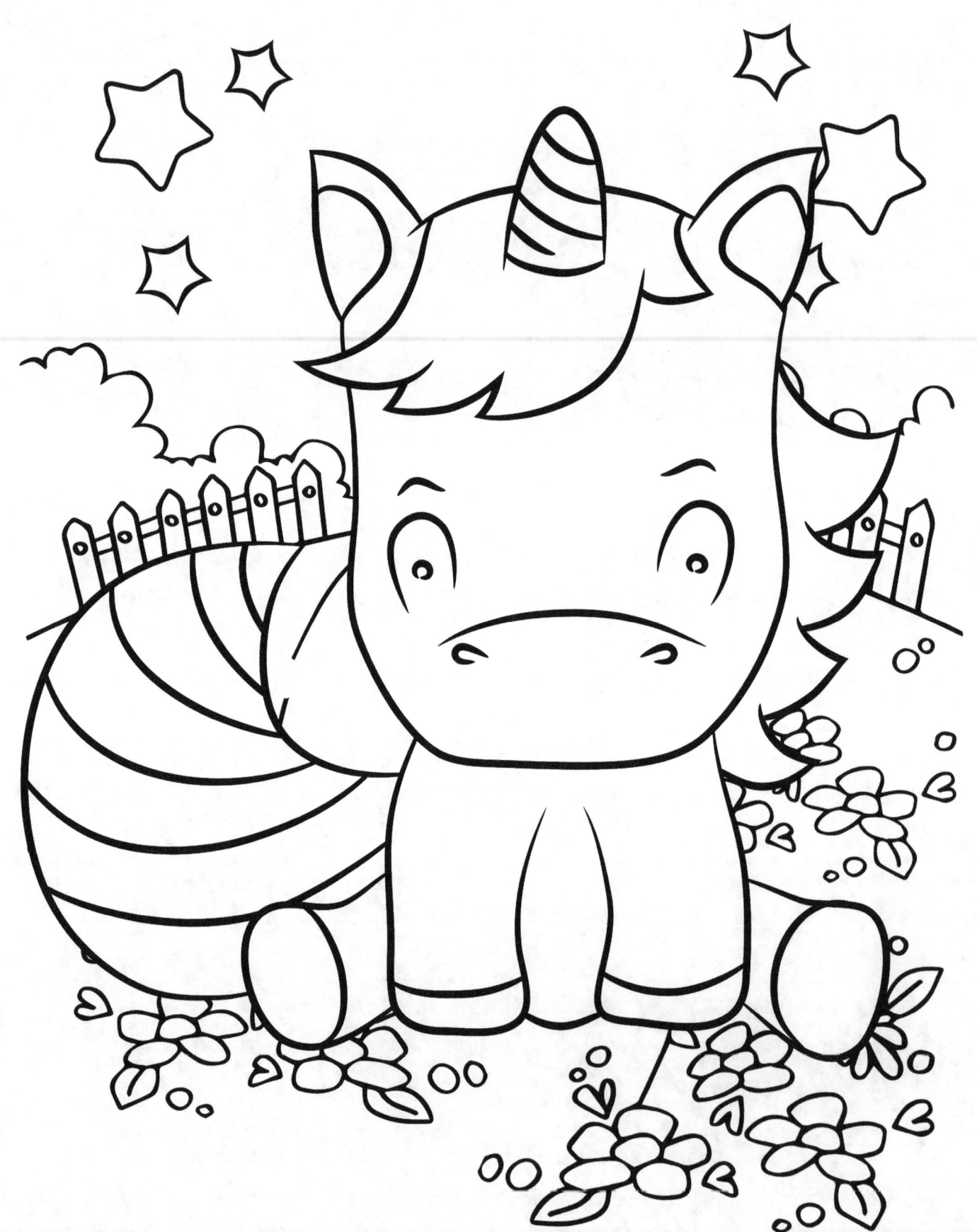

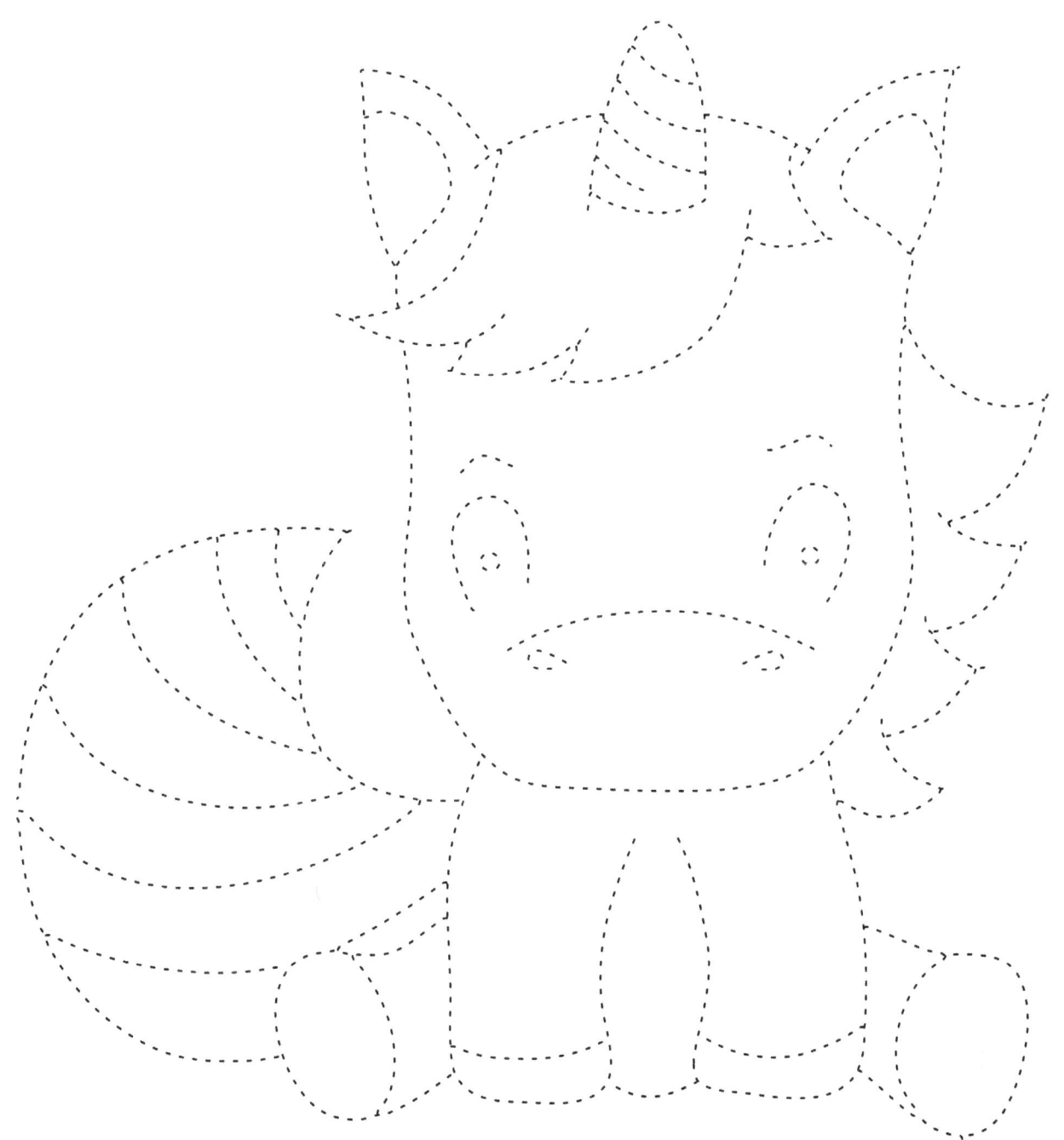

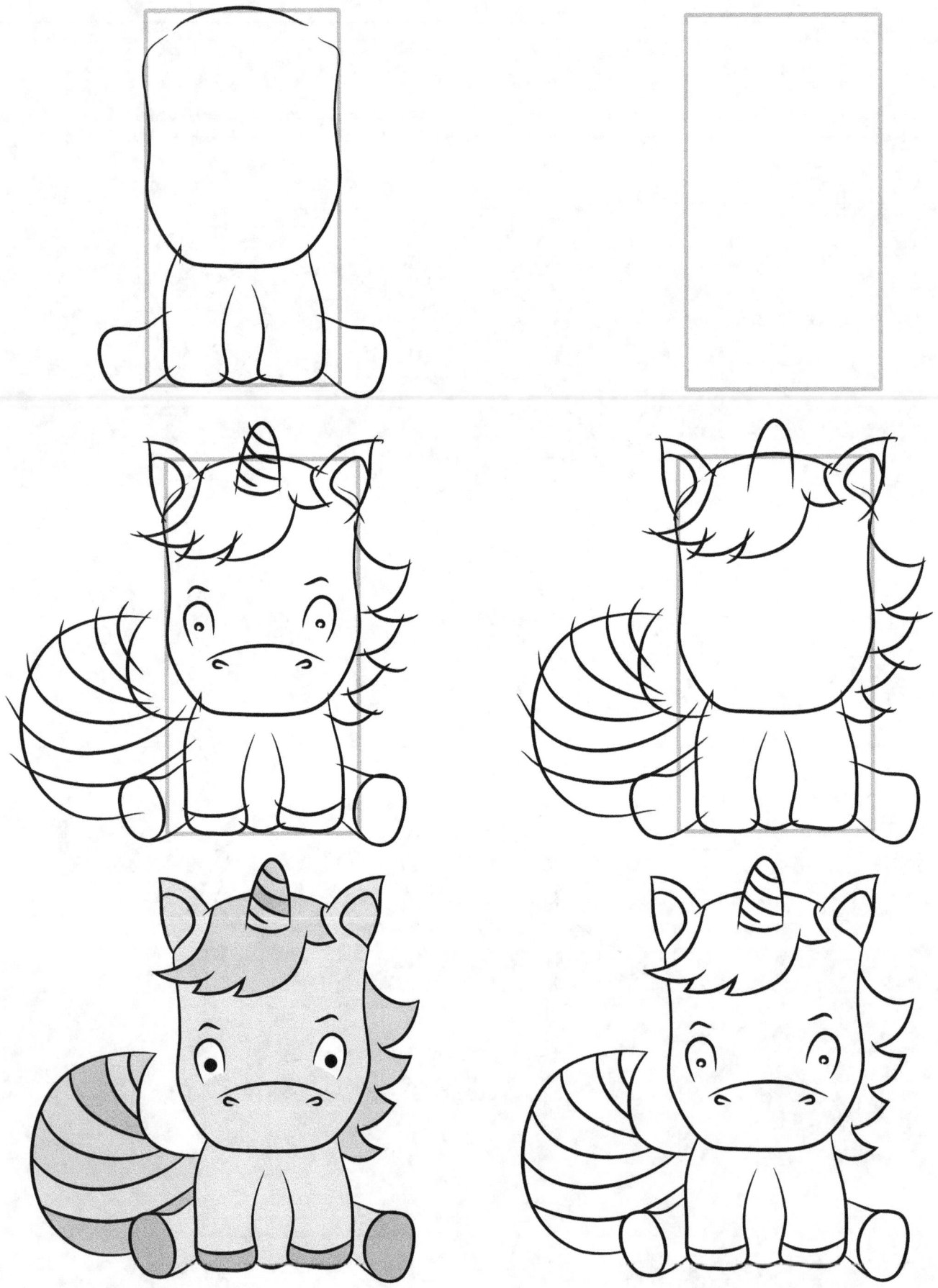

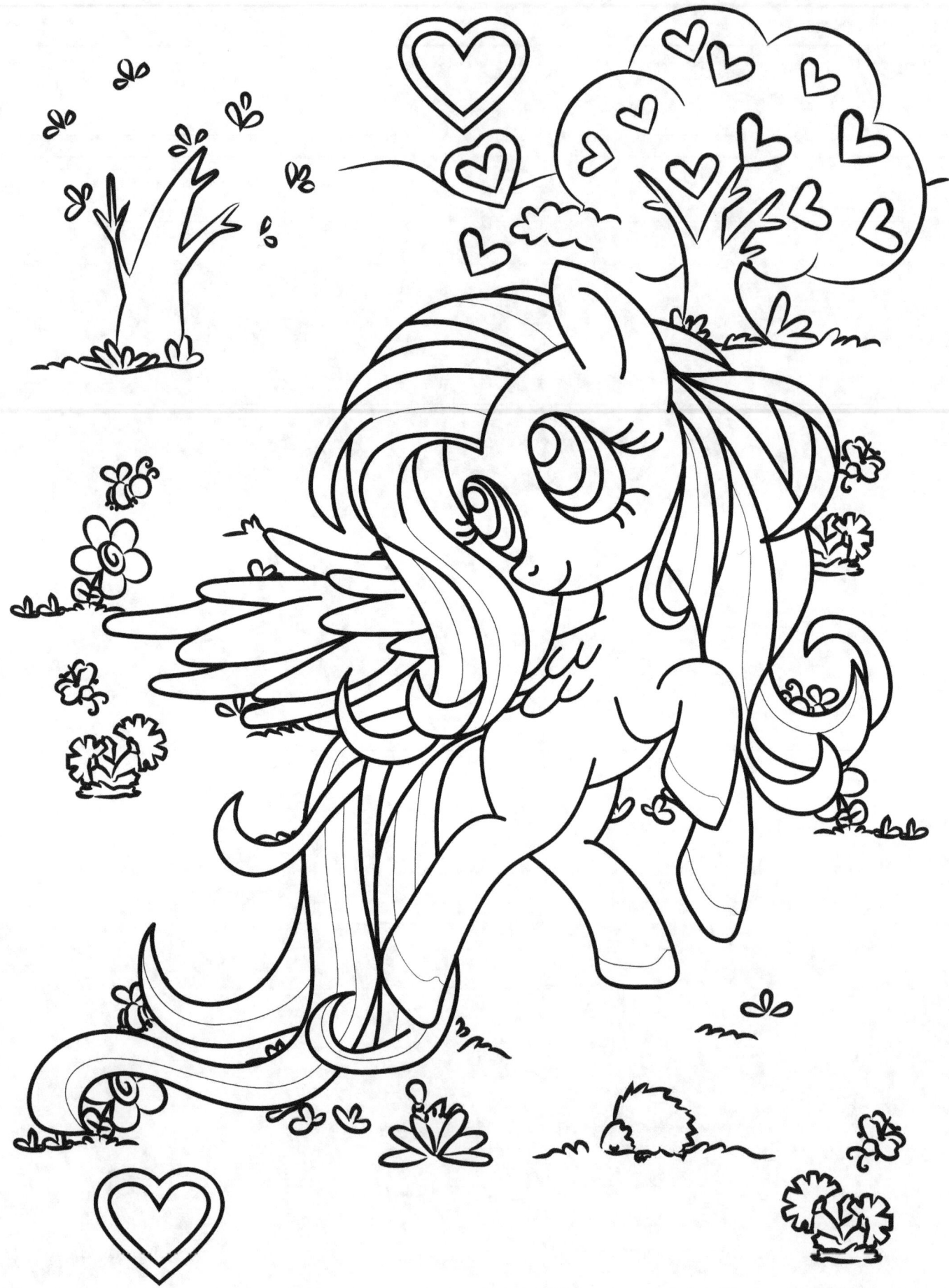

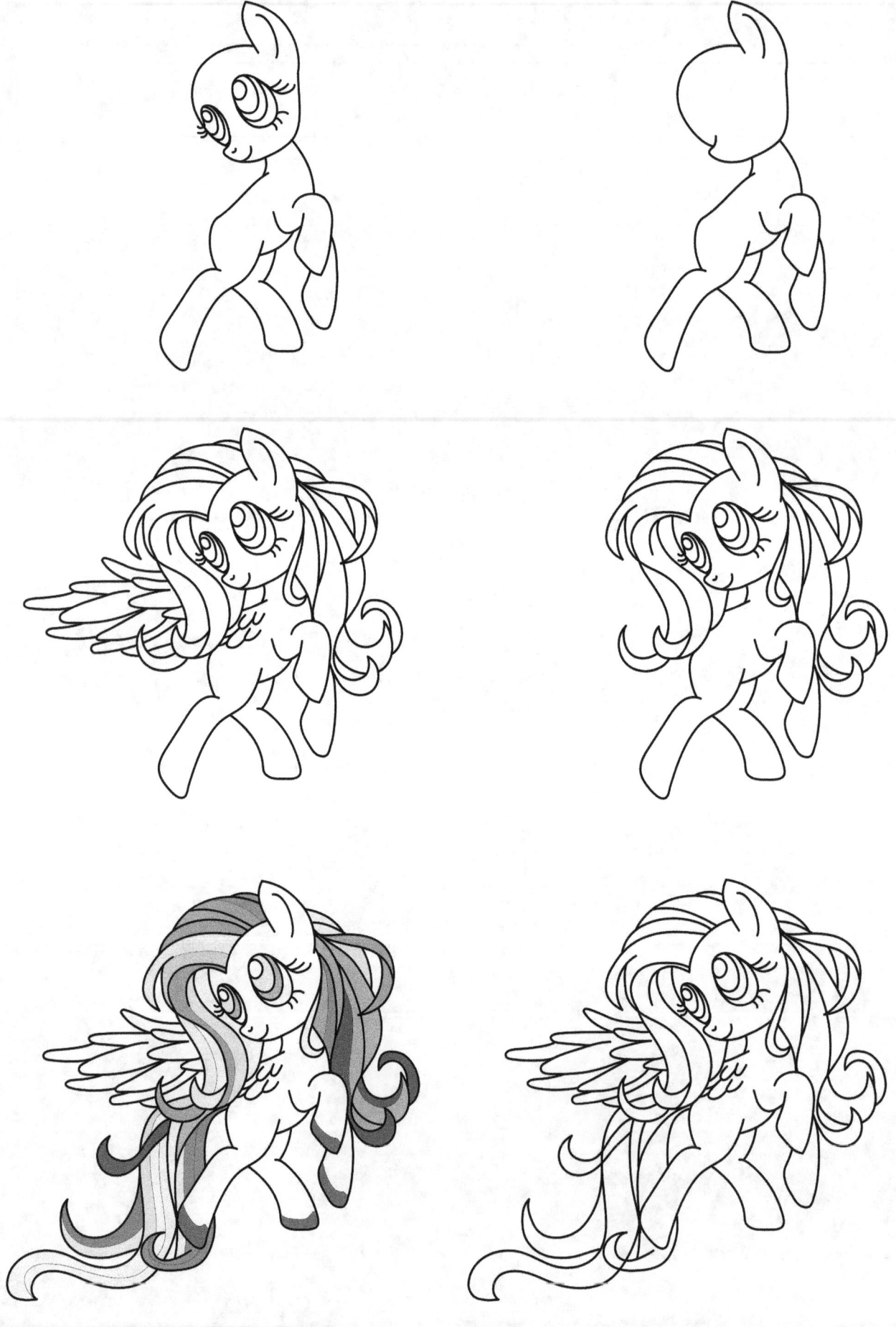

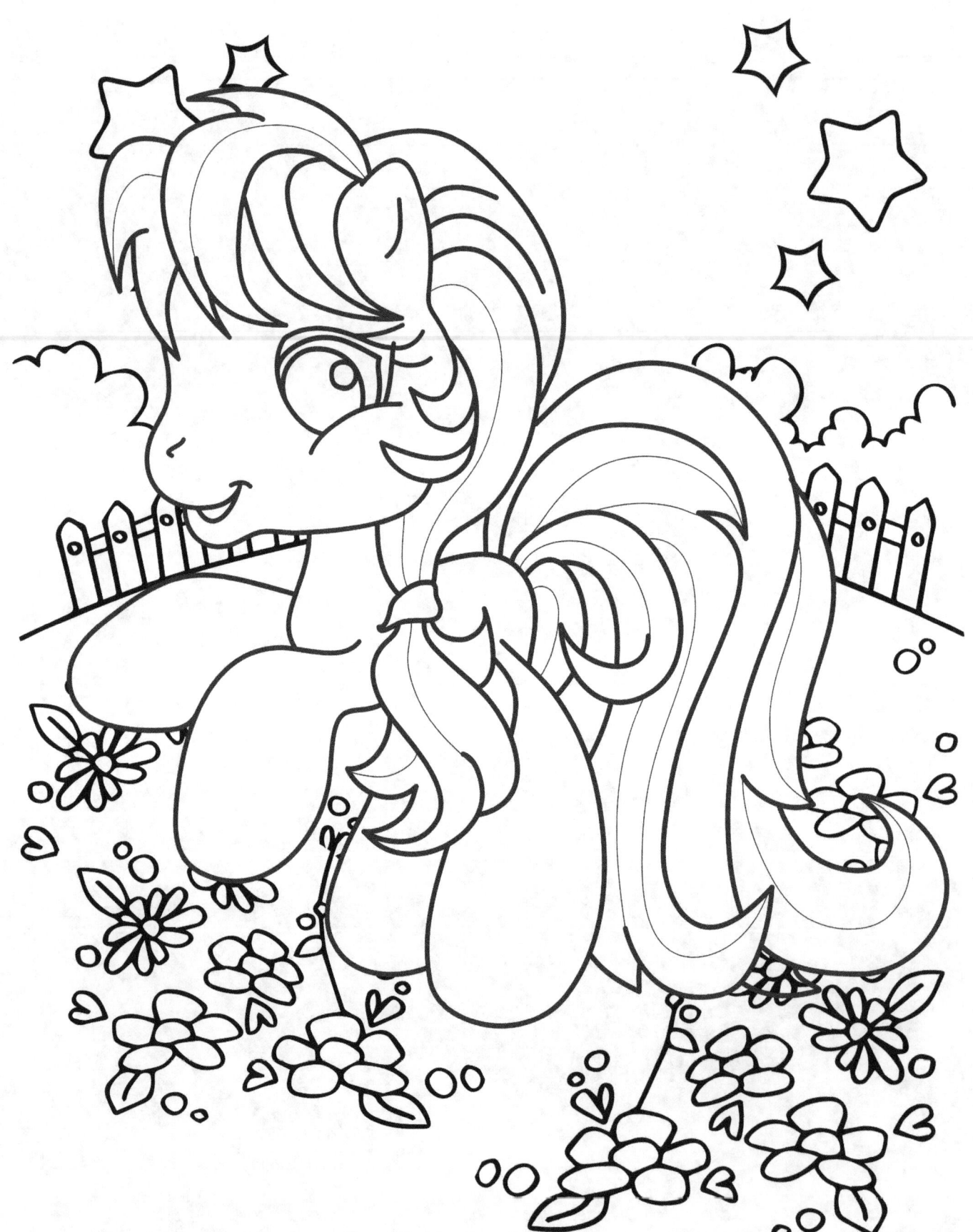

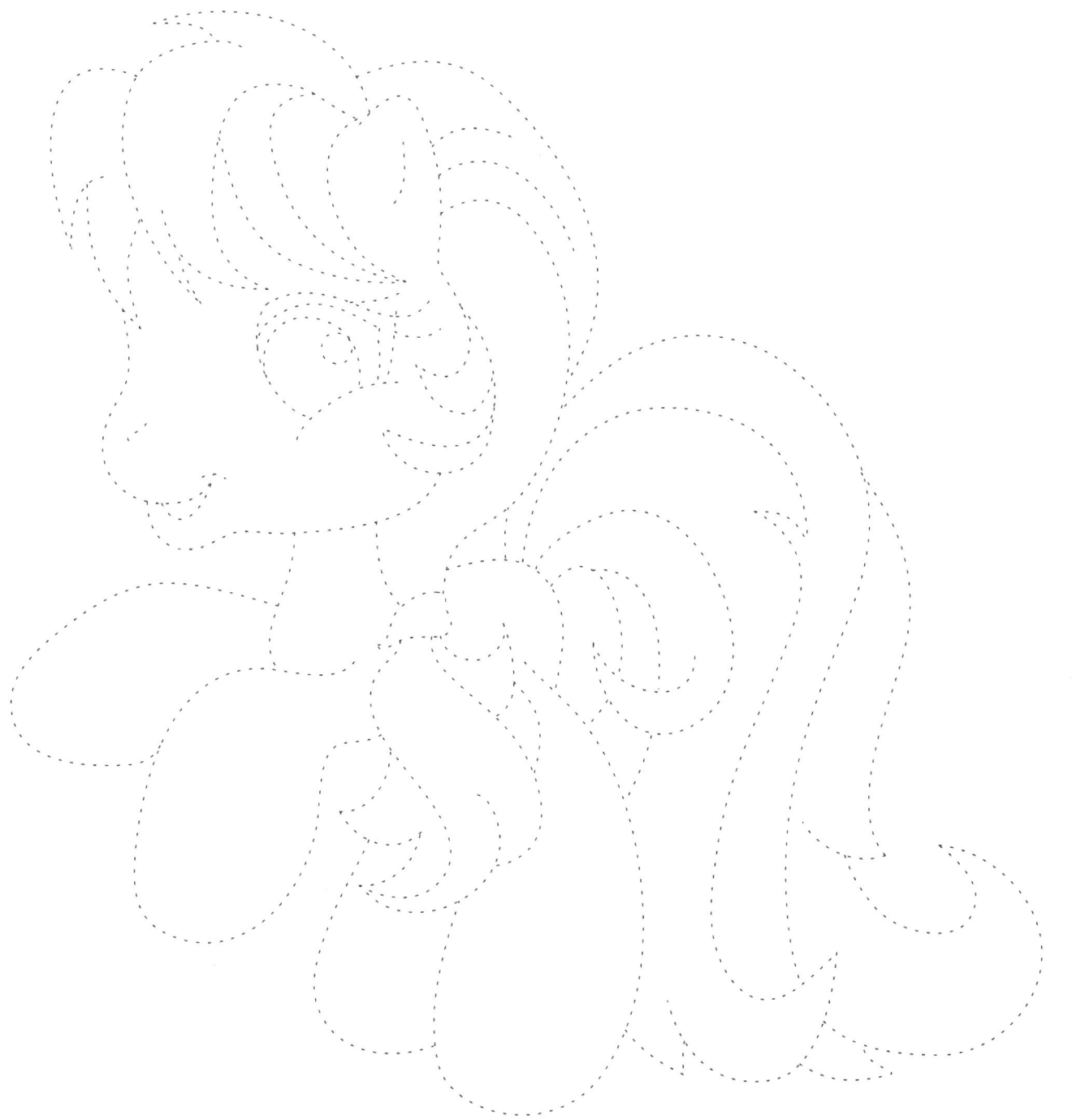

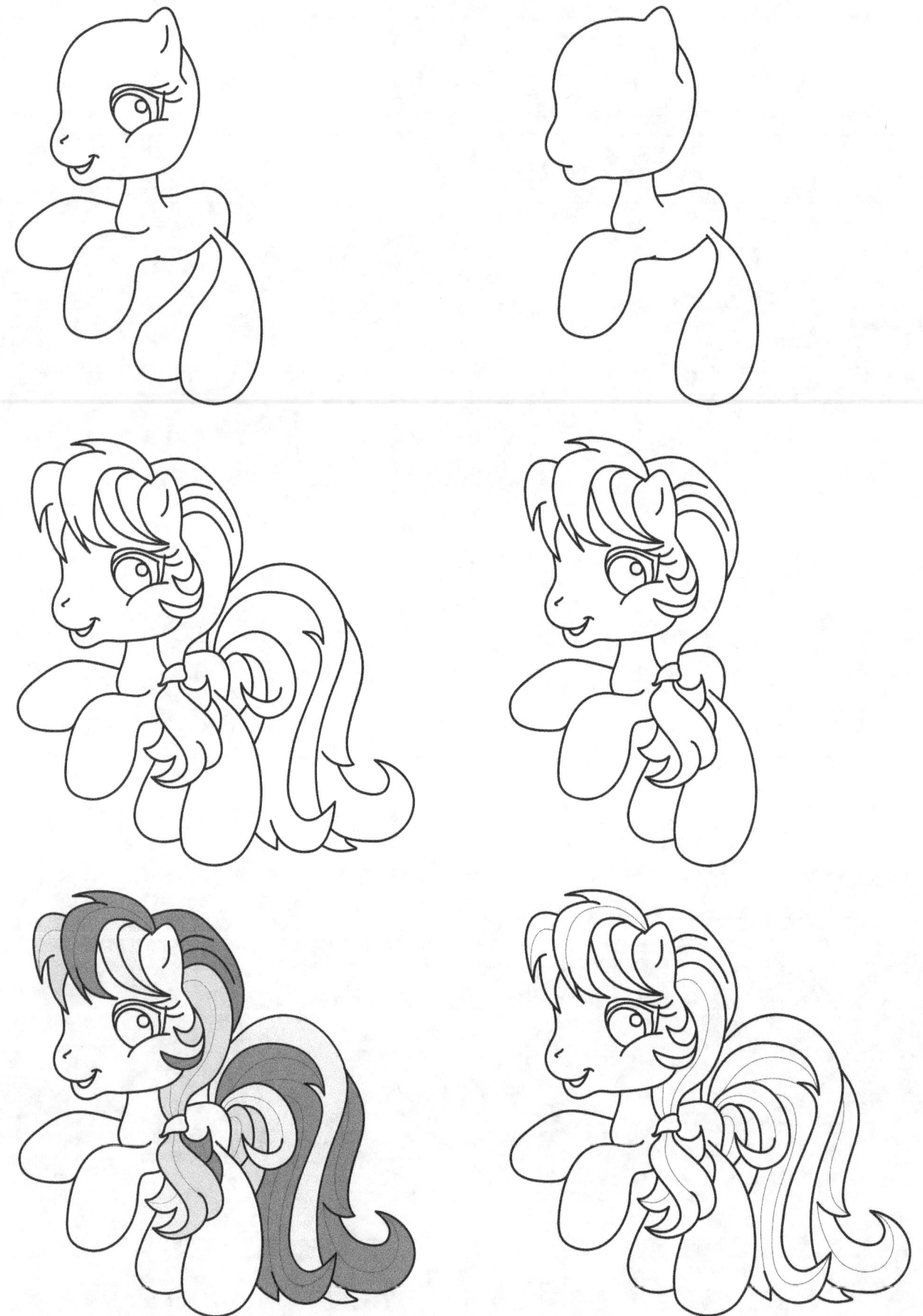

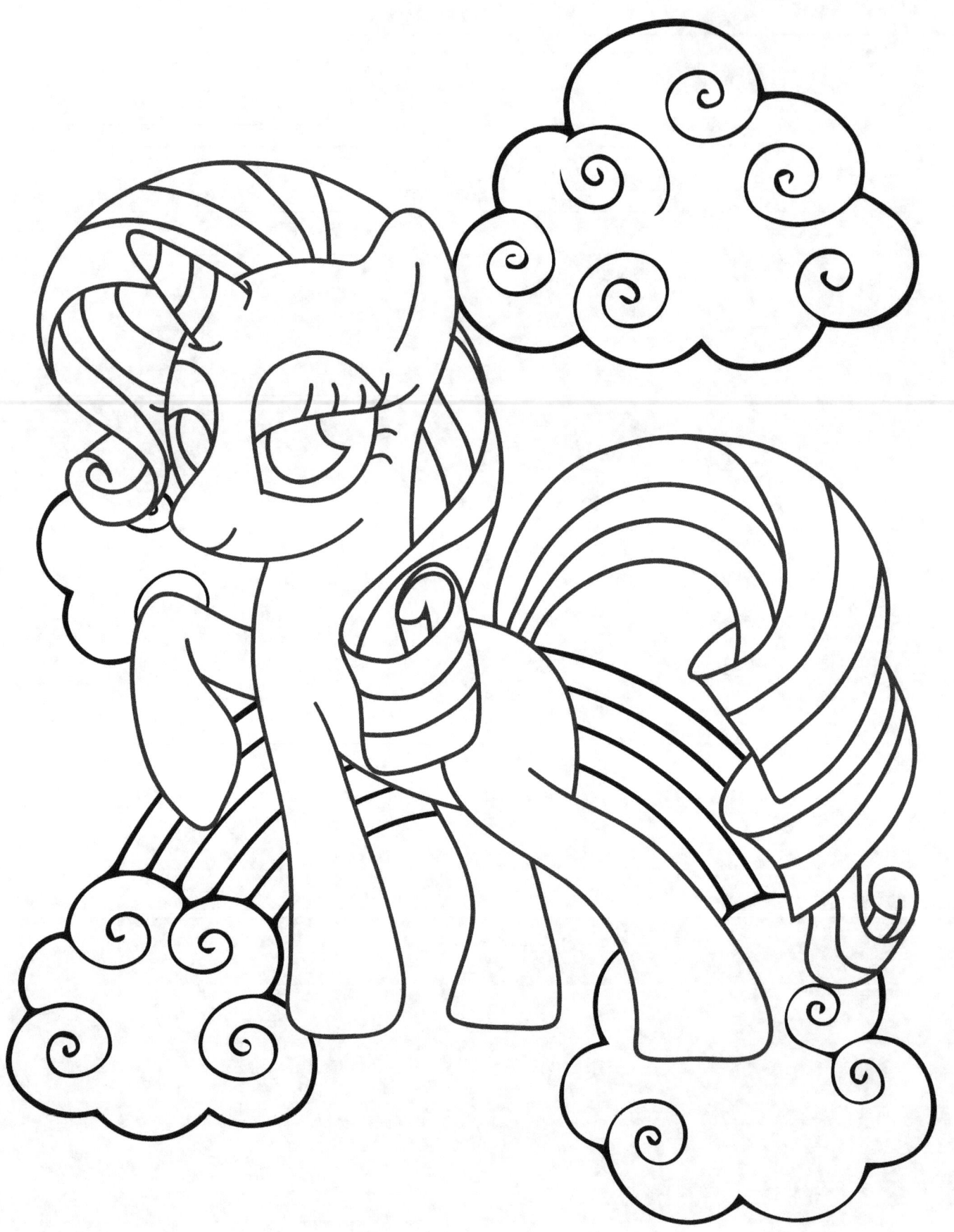

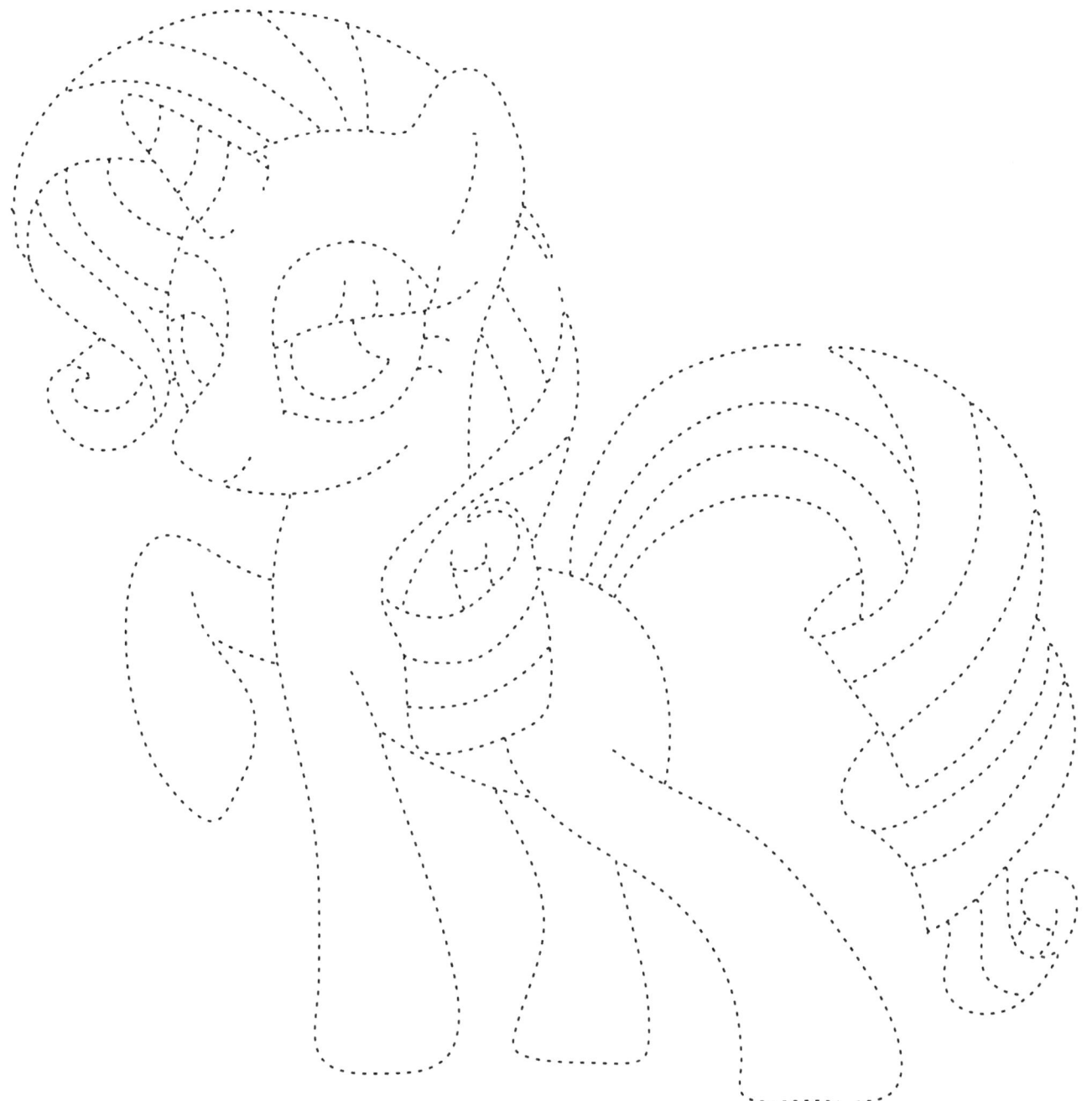

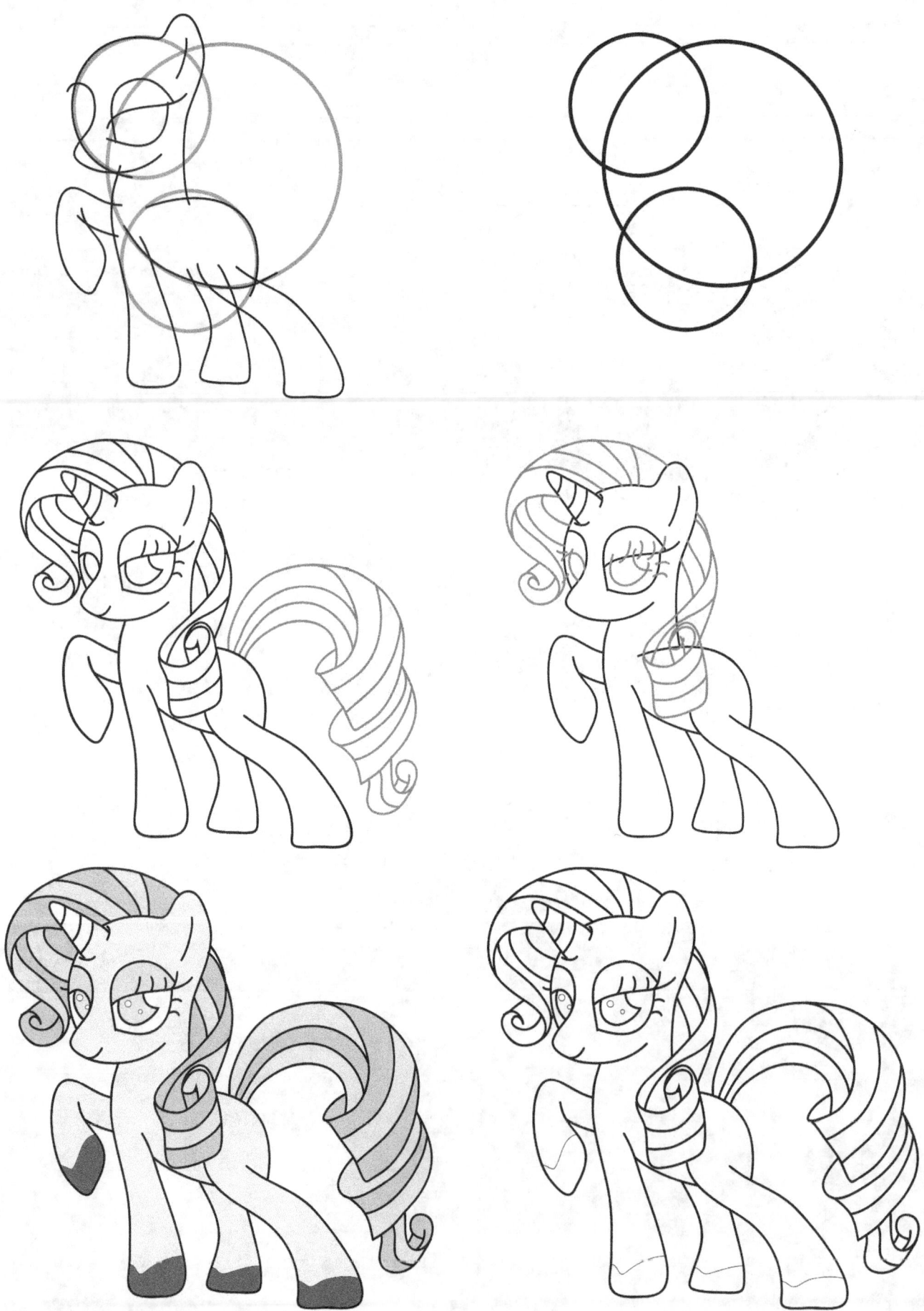

HOW TO DRAW CUTE UNICORNS

CUTE UNICORNS FOR LEARN TO DRAW

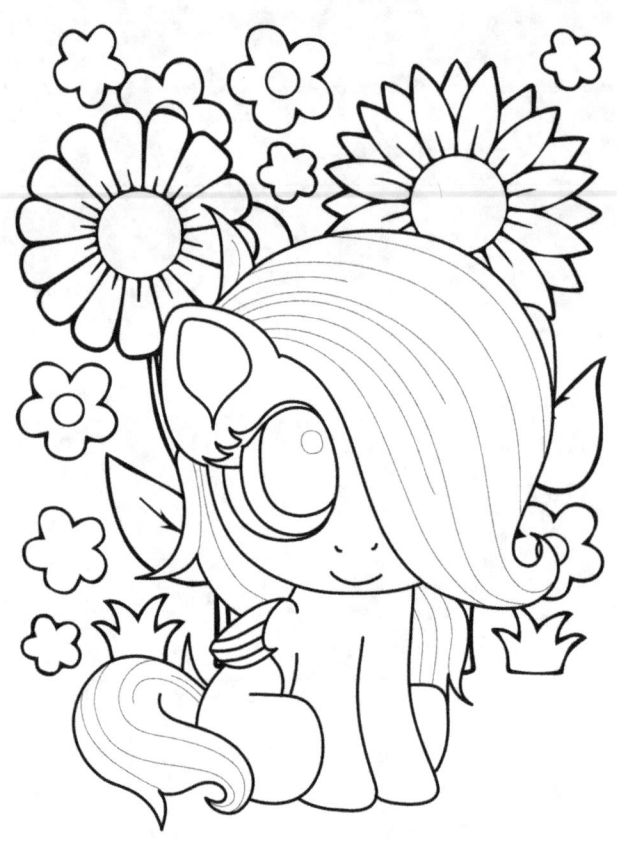

CUTE

FOR DRAWING

NEXT EDITION

COMONG SOON